Duncan has been involved within the security industry for over 15 years. He has held many roles within this industry from gatehouse to research and development sites. He has qualifications in advanced security management and has a general passion for the security industry.

Within this timeframe, Duncan has seen many changes, both good and bad.

I wish to dedicate this book to my wife, Mrs Nadyne Ashwell, as without her inspiration, encouragement and help, I wouldn't have got this done.

So, thank you, my love.

Duncan Ashwell

A BASIC SECURITY THOUGHT

AUSTIN MACAULEY PUBLISHERS™

LONDON * CAMBRIDGE * NEW YORK * SHARJAH

A CIP catalogue record for this title is available from the British Library.

ISBN 9781035842803 (Paperback)
ISBN 9781035842810 (ePub e-book)

www.austinmacauley.com

First Published 2024
Austin Macauley Publishers Ltd®
1 Canada Square
Canary Wharf
London
E14 5AA

I want to thank Austin Macauley Publishers for taking the chance on publishing my book.

Table of Contents

Hello, can I start with a thank you, for taking the time to have a look at my book on my take on the needs for the UK security industry.

Now, a bit about me the person behind this basic look and changes for the UK security industry.

My name is Duncan Ashwell. I have been in the security industry for over 14 years now, and I worked on many different types of security sites, from HMCTS, R&D, MOD, gatehouse, transport, shops and others.

As a security officer in the UK, the SIA has done a lot to help the security industry, but it still lays at the feet of the security companies to make the security industry the best it should be, on the goal to make the security industry an industry that has a good career path and a work to life balance.

Security companies should have the goal to keep standards high overall, and to make sure at the security offices are at the highest standards.

I have put some of the things that I think need to be looked at by the SIA and security companies, not only to improve on but to make a standard in the security industry.

This book is for security companies and security officers to have as a starting point and to improve over their security career; for companies to set a minimum standard for the security industry.

Thank you for taking the time to read this, and I hope it gives you a topic to talk about with others.

Introduction to the World of UK Security

UK security refers to the measures, policies, and actions implemented by the United Kingdom to protect its citizens, borders, infrastructure, and interests from various threats and risks. It encompasses a wide range of areas, including national defence, intelligence, counterterrorism, cybersecurity, border control, law enforcement, and emergency response.

The United Kingdom has a long history of prioritising security due to its geopolitical position, global influence, and its commitment to ensuring the safety and well-being of its population. The country faces diverse security challenges, including terrorism, organised crime, cyberattacks, geopolitical tensions, and potential threats to critical infrastructure.

National security is primarily the responsibility of the UK government, with various agencies and departments playing crucial roles in safeguarding the country. The Ministry of Defence oversees the nation's armed forces and defence strategy, while the intelligence community, including agencies like MI5 (Security Service) and MI6 (Secret Intelligence Service), focuses on gathering intelligence and countering threats to national security.

Counterterrorism efforts in the UK are led by the police, intelligence agencies, and specialised units such as the Counter Terrorism Command. These entities work together to prevent, investigate, and respond to terrorist incidents, ensuring public safety and protecting national security.

Cybersecurity is another critical aspect of UK security, given the increasing reliance on digital infrastructure and the potential for cyberattacks. The National Cyber Security Centre (NCSC) is responsible for protecting the country's digital systems, providing guidance, and responding to cyber threats.

Border security and immigration control are crucial for managing the flow of people and goods into the country. The UK Border Force, part of the Home Office, ensures the integrity of the UK's borders, enforces immigration and customs laws, and prevents the entry of individuals who pose a risk to national security.

In summary, UK security encompasses a comprehensive range of measures aimed at protecting the United Kingdom from various threats, both domestically and internationally. It involves defence, intelligence, counterterrorism, cybersecurity, border control, and law enforcement efforts, all working together to safeguard the nation, its people, and its interests.

UK security encompasses various measures and institutions that work together to safeguard the nation's interests, protect its citizens, and maintain peace and stability. These efforts span a wide range of areas, including defence, intelligence, law enforcement, cybersecurity, and border control. Here are some key aspects and ways in which the UK ensures security:

Defence: The UK maintains a strong military capability consisting of the British Army, Royal Navy, and Royal Air Force. These forces are responsible for defending the country against external threats, conducting peacekeeping missions, and providing support in times of national emergencies.

Intelligence Agencies: The UK has several intelligence agencies that gather information, analyse threats, and provide intelligence to support national security. The main agencies are MI5 (Security Service), responsible for counterintelligence and counterterrorism within the UK; MI6 (Secret Intelligence Service), focused on gathering intelligence abroad; and GCHQ (Government Communications Headquarters), responsible for signals intelligence and cybersecurity.

Law Enforcement: The UK has a robust law enforcement system that maintains public order, prevents and investigates crimes, and upholds the rule of law. The primary law enforcement agencies include the Metropolitan Police Service (Scotland Yard) in London and various regional police forces across the country.

Border Control: The UK Border Force is responsible for securing the UK's borders and managing immigration and customs. They enforce immigration laws, conduct passport checks, and prevent illegal entry into the country. Additionally, the security services collaborate with international partners to monitor and address potential security threats at borders.

Counterterrorism: The UK faces an ongoing threat from terrorism, and significant efforts are made to prevent and respond to such acts. These include intelligence gathering, surveillance, disrupting terrorist networks, and implementing counterterrorism legislation to detect and prosecute individuals involved in terrorist activities.

Cybersecurity: With the increasing reliance on technology, the UK places great emphasis on cybersecurity. The National Cyber Security Centre (NCSC) is the country's authority on cybersecurity, providing guidance, support, and incident response to protect against cyber threats, including hacking, malware, and cyber espionage.

International Cooperation: The UK collaborates closely with international partners, particularly through alliances like NATO, the Five Eyes intelligence-sharing network (comprising the UK, USA, Canada, Australia, and New Zealand), and the European Union (prior to Brexit). These partnerships allow for information sharing, joint operations, and coordinated responses to security challenges.

Legislation and Policies: The UK has enacted various laws and policies to enhance security and counter emerging threats. These include counterterrorism legislation, data protection laws, and initiatives to combat organised crime, human trafficking, and cyber threats. The government continually reviews and updates these measures to address evolving security risks.

It's important to note that the above is a general introduction to the ways of UK security, and specific operational details, strategies, and policies may not be publicly disclosed due to their sensitive nature.

The SIA (Security Industry Authority) is a non-departmental public body in the United Kingdom that is responsible for regulating the private security industry. The SIA was established under the Private Security Industry Act 2001 and became fully operational in 2004.

The primary purpose of the SIA is to raise standards and improve the professionalism of the private security industry in the UK. It does this by setting standards for licensing and qualifications for security personnel, as well as regulating the conduct of security companies.

The SIA issues licences to individuals who work in the private security industry, such as door supervisors, security guards, and CCTV operators. To obtain a licence, an individual must undergo training and pass a criminal record check.

The SIA also has the power to revoke or suspend licences if the holder breaches the standards of conduct or is found guilty of a criminal offence.

Overall, the SIA plays an essential role in ensuring the safety and security of the public by regulating the private security industry and maintaining high standards of professionalism and conduct.

Purpose of Security Companies

Security companies in the UK serve various purposes related to ensuring safety, protection, and risk management. Their primary objective is to provide security services to individuals, businesses, organisations, and government entities. Here are some common purposes of security companies in the UK:

Manned Guarding: Security companies often provide trained security personnel, such as security guards, to protect property, assets, and individuals. These guards may be stationed at entrances, conduct patrols, monitor surveillance systems, and enforce security protocols.

Event Security: Security companies are frequently hired to provide security services for events such as concerts, sports matches, conferences, and festivals. They help maintain order, manage access control, handle crowd management, and respond to any security incidents or emergencies.

CCTV and Alarm Systems: Security companies offer installation, maintenance, and monitoring of closed-circuit television (CCTV) systems and alarm systems. They help deter criminal activities, detect breaches, and provide evidence in the event of incidents.

Mobile Patrols: Security companies may provide mobile patrol units that conduct regular patrols of properties or designated areas. These patrols help deter criminal activities, identify security vulnerabilities, and provide a rapid response to incidents.

Access Control: Security companies implement and manage access control systems that regulate entry to buildings, facilities, or specific areas. This can include technologies such as swipe cards, biometric systems, and visitor management solutions to ensure authorised personnel access and protect against unauthorised entry.

Security Consultancy: Some security companies offer consultancy services to assess security risks, develop security strategies, and implement comprehensive security solutions tailored to clients' needs. They may conduct security audits, provide risk assessments, and advise on security best practices.

Retail Security: Security companies may provide specialised services for the retail sector, such as loss prevention officers, store detectives, and uniformed security guards. Their role is to deter theft, prevent shoplifting, and maintain a safe shopping environment.

Cybersecurity: With the increasing threat of cybercrime, some security companies offer cybersecurity services to help protect organisations' digital assets and systems. They conduct vulnerability assessments, implement security measures, and provide incident response services to mitigate cyber threats.

It's important to note that the specific services offered by security companies may vary based on their expertise, specialisation, and client requirements.

Why Is Security Needed in the UK

Security is crucial in the UK, as it is in any country, for several reasons:

Protection of Citizens: The primary purpose of security measures is to ensure the safety and well-being of the population. The UK government has a responsibility to protect its citizens from various threats, including crime, terrorism, and other forms of violence. Security measures help deter criminal activities, maintain law and order, and provide a sense of safety to the public.

Counterterrorism: The UK faces an ongoing threat from terrorism, both domestic and international. Security measures are essential to detect, prevent, and respond to terrorist activities. The government works closely with law enforcement agencies, intelligence services, and other organisations to identify potential threats, gather intelligence, and take necessary actions to mitigate the risk of terrorist attacks.

National Defence: Security plays a vital role in safeguarding the UK's sovereignty and territorial integrity. The country needs to protect its borders, critical infrastructure, and sensitive information from foreign espionage and cyber threats. Security measures ensure the defence capabilities of the nation and contribute to its overall resilience.

Economic Stability: A secure environment is crucial for fostering economic growth and stability. Businesses and investors require a stable and secure environment to thrive. Adequate security measures, such as law enforcement, cybersecurity, and intellectual property protection, help create a favourable climate for economic activities, attract investments, and ensure the smooth functioning of businesses.

International Relations: The UK's security posture also affects its standing in the international community. By maintaining strong security measures, the UK demonstrates its commitment to global peace and stability. It collaborates with other nations on intelligence sharing, counterterrorism efforts, and addressing transnational crime, fostering international cooperation and partnerships.

Public Confidence: Security measures help maintain public confidence in the government and its ability to protect its citizens. When people feel safe and secure, they are more likely to participate actively in society, engage in economic activities, and contribute to the overall well-being of the nation.

It is important to note that security measures must strike a balance between protecting citizens and respecting individual rights and civil liberties. The UK government aims to maintain a balance that upholds security while ensuring the rights and freedoms of its citizens.

Why the SIA Is Needed in the UK

The acronym "SIA" typically refers to the Security Industry Authority, which is the regulatory body responsible for overseeing the private security industry in the United Kingdom. The SIA was established under the Private Security Industry Act 2001 and has several important roles and functions:

Licensing: The SIA is responsible for licensing individuals who work in the private security industry. This includes security guards, door supervisors, CCTV operators, and other related roles. Licensing ensures that individuals working in the industry meet certain standards of training, competence, and professionalism.

Regulation: The SIA regulates the conduct of licensed individuals and security companies. They set standards of behaviour, ethics, and professional conduct to maintain public confidence in the private security industry. The SIA investigates complaints and takes appropriate actions against licence holders who breach the regulations.

Public Safety: The SIA's primary objective is to improve public safety. By regulating the industry and ensuring that individuals working in security roles meet specific standards, the SIA helps to ensure that private security personnel are capable of protecting people and property effectively.

Industry Standards: The SIA plays a vital role in establishing and maintaining standards within the private security industry. They work with relevant stakeholders to develop industry standards, codes of practice, and training requirements. This helps to raise the overall professionalism and quality of services provided by security personnel.

Compliance and Enforcement: The SIA has enforcement powers to take action against individuals and companies operating outside the law. They work closely with law enforcement agencies to tackle criminal activity, such as unlicensed security operations or individuals involved in illegal practices.

Overall, the SIA plays a crucial role in ensuring the integrity, professionalism, and safety of the private security industry in the UK. By licensing, regulating, and setting standards, they help maintain public confidence in the industry and protect the interests of both clients and the general public.

What the SIA Shouldn't
Be Used for in the UK

While the Security Industry Authority (SIA) plays an important role in regulating and licensing the private security industry in the UK, it is not designed to replace the functions and responsibilities of the UK police. Here are several reasons why the SIA should not be used as a replacement for the police:

Different Roles and Mandates: The SIA focuses on regulating and licensing private security operatives and businesses. Its primary goal is to ensure that individuals working in the private security industry meet certain standards and qualifications. On the other hand, the police have a much broader mandate, which includes maintaining public order, preventing and detecting crimes, and upholding the rule of law.

Law Enforcement Powers: The police have extensive powers granted by law, such as the power to arrest, detain, and conduct criminal investigations. These powers are essential for the effective maintenance of law and order. The SIA, on the other hand, does not possess similar powers and is not authorised to carry out law enforcement activities to the same extent as the police.

Community Policing and Trust: The police have a unique relationship with the communities they serve. They are responsible for engaging with the public, building trust, and addressing the specific needs and concerns of local communities. This community-oriented approach is critical for effective policing. The SIA, being a regulatory body, does not have the same level of community engagement and may not be as effective in fostering trust and cooperation.

Investigation and Intelligence Capabilities: The police are equipped with specialised resources, including dedicated investigators, forensic experts, and intelligence units, to carry out complex investigations and gather intelligence on criminal activities. These capabilities are crucial for solving crimes and preventing future offences. The SIA, by contrast, primarily focuses on ensuring the competence and professionalism of private security personnel and does not possess the same level of investigative capacity.

Accountability and Oversight: The police are subject to a high level of accountability and oversight mechanisms, such as independent police complaints commissions, internal affairs departments, and judicial review processes. These mechanisms help ensure transparency, fairness, and adherence to legal standards. While the SIA has its own regulatory framework, it does not have the same level of independent oversight and accountability structures as the police.

It is important to recognise that the SIA and the police serve different roles and functions within the UK's criminal justice system. While the SIA provides regulation and licensing for the private security industry, the police are responsible for maintaining public safety, enforcing the law, and upholding order in society.

While it is important to recognise that every situation can have its own unique factors and considerations, there are a few reasons why UK security officers should not view themselves as police officers.

Different Roles and Authority: Security officers and police officers have distinct roles and authority levels. Security officers are responsible for the protection of people and property within a specific area, such as a private establishment, while police officers have a broader mandate to enforce the law, maintain public order, and investigate crimes. Their training, powers, and legal authorities differ significantly.

Legal Limitations: Security officers have limited legal powers compared to police officers. They do not have the authority to arrest or detain individuals beyond the scope of a citizen's arrest. Engaging in activities beyond their legal powers can lead to legal liabilities for security officers and the organisations they represent.

Training and Qualifications: Police officers undergo extensive training and meet specific qualifications to perform their duties effectively. They receive education on topics such as law enforcement tactics, criminal law, constitutional rights, conflict resolution, and community policing. While security officers may receive training specific to their role, it typically does not encompass the same breadth and depth as police officer training.

Accountability and Oversight: Police officers operate under a structured system of accountability and oversight. They are subject to internal affairs investigations, independent police oversight bodies, and a code of conduct. Security officers, on the other hand, are accountable primarily to their employers and may not have the same level of external scrutiny. It is important for security officers to understand the boundaries of their authority and responsibilities to ensure ethical conduct.

Public Perception and Trust: The public perception of police officers and security officers differs due to their distinct roles and authority. Identifying as a police officer when one is not can lead to confusion and potentially erode public trust. Maintaining transparency about one's role as a security officer and engaging with the public in a manner appropriate to that role helps build trust and foster positive relationships.

In summary, it is crucial for security officers to recognise and embrace their specific role and authority within the framework of the law. This distinction ensures clarity, accountability, and effective collaboration with law enforcement agencies when necessary.

There can be several reasons why it might be considered a bad idea for UK security companies to offer to perform the role of the police. Here are a few potential concerns:

Accountability and Oversight: The police force is a public institution with a system of checks and balances in place to ensure accountability and transparency. Private security companies operate for profit and may prioritise their clients' interests over public safety. Transferring law enforcement responsibilities to private entities could raise concerns about the lack of public oversight and potential abuses of power.

Conflict of Interest: Private security companies often work for specific clients or industries and have contractual obligations to prioritise their clients' interests. This arrangement could lead to conflicts of interest when enforcing the law. The police, on the other hand, are expected to serve and protect the public without bias.

Training and Expertise: The police undergo rigorous training and education to develop the necessary skills and knowledge for law enforcement. While security companies may provide valuable services, their training and expertise may not match the comprehensive training received by police officers. Police officers are trained in a wide range of areas, including criminal law, community policing, conflict resolution, and de-escalation techniques.

Consistency and Standards: The police force operates under a framework of established laws, regulations, and protocols. This ensures consistency in the application of justice and the protection of individual rights. Private security companies may have different standards and procedures, potentially leading to inconsistencies in how the law is enforced.

Public Trust and Legitimacy: Policing is a public service that relies on the trust and cooperation of the community. Handing over law enforcement responsibilities to private companies could undermine public trust in the justice system. The public may question the motivations and impartiality of private security companies, potentially eroding confidence in the fairness and legitimacy of law enforcement.

It is important to note that some countries do employ private security companies for certain tasks, such as guarding specific facilities or providing additional support in high-risk areas. However, completely replacing the police force with private security companies would pose significant challenges and raise fundamental questions about the nature of law enforcement and public safety.

SIA Licences Need Changes

Combining the door supervisor and security guarding SIA (Security Industry Authority) licences into a single licence in the UK can offer several benefits:

Streamlined Training: By merging the licenses, the training process can be streamlined, making it more efficient and cost-effective. Instead of individuals needing to obtain separate licences for different security roles, they can undergo a comprehensive training program that covers the necessary skills and knowledge required for both door supervision and security guarding.

Flexibility and Adaptability: A single licence would provide security professionals with greater flexibility and adaptability in their roles. They would be equipped with the skills and qualifications to work in various security positions, depending on the requirements of different venues or events. This would enhance their employability and make it easier for them to transition between different security roles.

Increased Pool of Qualified Professionals: Combining the licenses would likely lead to an increase in the number of qualified professionals available in the security industry. This expanded pool of talent can help address any shortages of skilled security personnel and ensure that venues and events have access to well-trained individuals capable of handling different security responsibilities effectively.

Improved Public Safety: The security industry plays a crucial role in ensuring public safety and maintaining order in various settings. By merging the licenses, there is potential for enhanced training and standards across the industry. This could result in a higher level of professionalism and competency among security personnel, leading to improved safety and security for the public.

Administrative Simplification: From an administrative perspective, consolidating the licenses can simplify the licensing process. It would reduce the complexity of managing multiple licences, both for the licensing authority and the individuals seeking licensure. This streamlining could lead to a more efficient and effective licensing system overall.

It's important to note that these are potential advantages, and any decision to merge licences would require careful consideration of various factors, including consultation with industry stakeholders, assessing potential challenges, and ensuring that the training and standards remain robust.

The decision of whether the Security Industry Authority (SIA) should get rid of non-frontline licences in the UK is subjective and can depend on various factors. While I can provide you with some potential arguments for and against this proposition, it's important to note that the SIA's policies and regulations may have evolved beyond my knowledge cutoff in September 2021. I recommend checking the latest information from official sources to obtain the most accurate and up-to-date information.

Reasons in favour of getting rid of non-frontline licences:

Focus on Public Safety: By eliminating non-frontline licences, the SIA can prioritise resources and efforts towards ensuring the safety and security of the general public. This could allow them to allocate more attention and resources to roles directly involved in public-facing security activities.

Streamlined Regulation: Reducing the number of licence categories could simplify the regulatory framework for the security industry. A streamlined system may be easier to manage and enforce, leading to improved oversight and compliance.

Cost-Effectiveness: Consolidating licences could potentially lead to cost savings for both the SIA and security industry professionals. Fewer licence types would reduce administrative burdens and costs associated with maintaining multiple licences.

Enhanced Professionalism: By focusing on frontline security roles, the SIA can emphasise training and qualifications for those directly involved in public safety. This could contribute to raising the overall professionalism and standards of the industry, ensuring that individuals working in critical security positions possess appropriate skills and expertise.

Reasons against getting rid of non-frontline licences:

Diverse Security Roles: The security industry encompasses a wide range of specialised roles beyond frontline positions, such as supervisors, managers, consultants, and trainers. Removing non-frontline licences might hinder the ability of these professionals to perform their duties effectively, potentially leading to a gap in expertise and capabilities.

Risk Management: Some non-frontline roles, although not directly involved in public-facing activities, play crucial roles in managing risks, conducting investigations, and providing essential support to frontline security personnel. Eliminating these licences may result in a loss of valuable expertise and compromise overall security strategies.

Employment Opportunities: Removing non-frontline licences could potentially limit job opportunities for individuals who specialise in non-public-facing security roles. This may negatively impact employment prospects and career growth within the industry.

Regulatory Complexity: While streamlining licence categories may have administrative benefits, it could also create challenges in distinguishing and regulating various roles within the security industry. It may require careful consideration to ensure that essential functions are adequately accounted for under any revised licensing system.

Ultimately, the decision to eliminate non-frontline licences rests with the SIA and requires a careful assessment of various factors, including public safety, industry needs, regulatory efficiency, and stakeholder input.

The introduction of a security managers licence by the Security Industry Authority (SIA) in the UK can have several potential benefits. Here are a few reasons why such a licence may be beneficial:

Enhanced Professionalism: Implementing a security managers licence can raise the professional standards within the security industry. It would establish a recognised qualification and regulatory framework for security managers, ensuring they possess the necessary skills, knowledge, and experience to effectively manage security operations.

Quality Assurance: By introducing a licensing system, the SIA can ensure that security managers meet specific criteria and undergo appropriate training. This helps to guarantee a certain level of competence and expertise among security managers, leading to improved service quality and client satisfaction.

Standardisation: A licensing system facilitates standardisation across the security industry. It establishes consistent benchmarks for the required qualifications, experience, and ethical conduct of security managers. This promotes fairness and transparency in the hiring process and reduces the risk of unqualified or unsuitable individuals occupying management positions.

Public Safety and Security: Security managers play a crucial role in safeguarding public safety and security. By implementing a licensing system, the SIA can ensure that security managers have the necessary understanding of relevant laws, regulations, and best practices. This can contribute to more effective security strategies, emergency preparedness, and incident response, ultimately enhancing public safety.

Industry Reputation: A licensing system can help improve the overall reputation of the security industry. By setting high standards for security managers, the SIA can enhance the industry's credibility and trustworthiness. This can lead to increased confidence from clients, stakeholders, and the general public, attracting more businesses and opportunities for security service providers.

Professional Development: A licensing system can promote continuous professional development among security managers. It encourages individuals to stay updated with evolving security practices, technologies, and regulations through ongoing training and education. This, in turn, leads to a more competent and adaptable security workforce.

It is important to note that the introduction of a security managers licence would require careful planning, consultation, and collaboration with industry stakeholders to ensure its successful implementation and effectiveness.

The decision to implement a licence type overhaul by the UK Security Industry Authority (SIA) would depend on various factors and considerations. While I don't have information on specific developments since my knowledge cutoff in September 2021, I can provide you with some general reasons why an organisation like the SIA might consider a licence type overhaul:

Industry Adaptation: Over time, industries evolve and new security risks emerge. An overhaul of licence types can ensure that the SIA keeps pace with these changes and adapts its licensing framework to reflect the current security landscape.

Enhanced Regulatory Effectiveness: A licence type overhaul may aim to improve the effectiveness of regulatory measures. It could involve redefining licence categories, introducing new licensing requirements, or enhancing training and qualification standards to ensure that security personnel possess the necessary skills and knowledge to perform their duties effectively.

Streamlined Processes: Simplifying and streamlining the licence types can make it easier for individuals and organisations to navigate the licensing system.

This could include reducing administrative burdens, eliminating redundancies, or consolidating similar licence types into broader categories.

Alignment with International Standards: The SIA may consider a licence type overhaul to align its licensing framework with international standards or best practices in the security industry. This alignment can help improve consistency and facilitate recognition of UK-issued licences in other jurisdictions, potentially benefiting security professionals seeking work opportunities abroad.

Public Confidence and Trust: A licence type overhaul can contribute to building public confidence and trust in the security industry. By ensuring that licence types are relevant, comprehensive, and reflect the evolving nature of security threats, the SIA can enhance the credibility and professionalism of the industry.

Industry Consultation: The SIA might undertake a licence type overhaul after consulting with industry stakeholders, including security companies, trade associations, and professionals. Engaging with these stakeholders can provide valuable insights into industry needs and help shape an updated licensing framework that meets the requirements of both the industry and the public.

It's important to note that the specific rationale for a licence type overhaul by the UK SIA would depend on the unique circumstances, priorities, and challenges faced by the security industry in the UK at any given time. To obtain the most accurate and up-to-date information on the subject, it would be best to refer to official announcements or news from the SIA or related government bodies.

An overhaul of the SIA (Security Industry Authority) licences can have several potential benefits for the security industry. Here are a few reasons why such an overhaul could be advantageous:

Enhanced Professionalism: An overhaul can raise the overall professionalism and standards within the security industry. By implementing stricter requirements, such as increased training and qualification standards, the industry can ensure that security personnel possess the necessary skills and knowledge to perform their duties effectively. This can enhance the reputation of the industry as a whole.

Improved Public Trust: A comprehensive overhaul can contribute to building public trust and confidence in the security industry. By implementing rigorous licensing procedures, including thorough background checks and vetting processes, the industry can demonstrate its commitment to providing reliable and trustworthy security services. This can help alleviate concerns about the quality and reliability of security personnel.

Increased Competence: Updating and revising the licensing framework can help ensure that security professionals are up to date with the latest industry standards, technologies, and best practices. Regularly reviewing and adapting the licensing requirements can address emerging challenges and equip security personnel with the necessary skills to handle new security threats effectively.

Consistent Regulation: An overhaul can lead to a more consistent and standardised regulatory framework across the industry. This can help eliminate inconsistencies and discrepancies that may exist between different regions or sectors within the security industry. Consistent regulation allows for fair competition and a level playing field for security service providers.

Adaptability to Changing Needs: Overhauling the SIA licences can facilitate the industry's ability to adapt to evolving security needs. As new risks and technologies emerge, the licensing framework can be updated to address these changes. This ensures that security personnel have the required competencies and knowledge to handle emerging threats, such as cybercrime or advanced surveillance systems.

Enhanced Professional Development: A revised licensing system can encourage ongoing professional development among security personnel. By incorporating continuous training and skills upgrading requirements into the licensing process, the industry can promote a culture of lifelong learning and development. This benefits both individual security professionals and the industry as a whole by ensuring a highly skilled and capable workforce.

It's worth noting that the specific details and approach of an overhaul would need to be carefully considered to maximise its benefits and minimise any potential drawbacks. However, an effective overhaul can contribute to a more professional, trusted, and competent security industry, ultimately benefiting both service providers and the public.

Staff

There could be various reasons why security officers in the UK might switch jobs frequently. Some possible explanations include:

Limited Career Advancement Opportunities: The security industry may not always provide clear pathways for career progression or professional development. As a result, security officers may seek new job opportunities to gain higher positions, better pay, or more responsibilities.

Better Employment Offers: Security officers may receive job offers from other companies or organisations that provide more favourable working conditions, improved benefits, or higher wages. They may choose to switch jobs to enhance their overall job satisfaction and financial well-being.

Dissatisfaction with Current Employment: Security officers might leave their current jobs due to dissatisfaction with their work environment, management, or job-related policies. If they feel undervalued, experience conflicts, or encounter other job-related issues, they may seek alternative employment.

Seasonal or Temporary Work: Some security roles are inherently temporary or contract-based, such as event security or short-term assignments. In these cases, security officers may switch jobs frequently as they move between different temporary opportunities based on demand or availability.

Personal Preferences and Variety: Some security officers may simply enjoy the variety of experiences that come with working in different environments. By switching jobs, they can work in various settings, such as retail, residential, corporate, or event security, which can provide them with different challenges and experiences.

Industry-Specific Factors: Certain industries, such as construction or industrial sites, may have specific security requirements that require officers to move between projects or sites. These officers may switch jobs to align with new projects or to meet changing security needs in their sector.

It's important to note that while frequent job switching may be common in the security industry, it is not necessarily the case for all security officers in the UK. Individual motivations and circumstances can vary significantly.

To keep staff and make security officers valued in the UK, companies can consider implementing the following strategies:

Competitive Compensation: Offer competitive salaries and benefits packages to attract and retain talented security officers. Conduct market research to ensure that the compensation offered is in line with industry standards.

Career Development Opportunities: Provide opportunities for professional growth and development. This can include training programs, certifications, and advancement opportunities within the security department or the company as a whole.

Recognition and Appreciation: Regularly recognise and appreciate the efforts of security officers. Acknowledge their contributions to the company's safety and security and publicly commend exceptional performance.

Safe and Supportive Work Environment: Foster a safe and supportive work environment for security officers. Provide them with necessary resources, equipment, and tools to perform their duties effectively. Address any concerns they may have promptly and ensure their physical and emotional well-being.

Employee Engagement: Involve security officers in decision-making processes and encourage their active participation. Seek their feedback and ideas on improving security protocols and procedures. Regularly communicate organisational goals and objectives to make them feel part of the company's overall mission.

Professional Recognition: Promote the importance of the security officer role within the organisation and society. Highlight the value they bring in safeguarding people, assets, and information. Recognise security officers' achievements through internal and external awards and industry certifications.

Continuous Training and Education: Provide ongoing training and education opportunities to enhance the skills and knowledge of security officers. This can include technical skills, emergency response training, customer service training, and the latest security trends and technologies.

Team-Building and Collaboration: Encourage teamwork and collaboration among security officers and with other departments. Organise team-building activities and promote a sense of camaraderie to foster a positive work culture.

Regular Performance Reviews: Conduct regular performance reviews to assess security officers' performance, provide constructive feedback, and set goals for improvement. This can help them understand their strengths and areas for development.

Employee Assistance Programs: Offer employee assistance programs that provide support for security officers' personal and professional challenges. This can include counselling services, financial advice, or work-life balance programs.

By implementing these strategies, companies can create an environment where security officers feel valued, motivated, and engaged, leading to increased job satisfaction and improved staff retention.

There are several reasons why it is argued that security companies should stop offering zero-hour contracts in the UK. Here are a few key points:

Job Insecurity: Zero-hour contracts provide little to no job security for workers. Employees on such contracts have no guarantee of consistent working hours, which makes it difficult for them to plan their finances and meet their basic needs. It can lead to income instability and increased stress.

Unpredictable Income: Without fixed working hours, employees on zero-hour contracts often face fluctuating incomes. It becomes challenging for them to budget effectively, pay bills, and plan for the future. This can result in financial hardship and contribute to overall economic inequality.

Limited Employment Rights: Zero-hour contracts often deprive workers of essential employment rights. Employees on these contracts may have limited access to benefits such as sick pay, holiday pay, and maternity/paternity leave. They may also face difficulties in accessing loans or mortgages due to the lack of stable income.

Exploitative Practices: Some argue that zero-hour contracts can facilitate exploitative employment practices. Employers may exploit the flexibility of these contracts by demanding workers to be available at short notice, sometimes without providing adequate compensation for the inconvenience. This imbalance of power can lead to the mistreatment of workers.

Negative Impact on Well-Being: The uncertainty and lack of control over working hours can have a detrimental impact on workers' physical and mental well-being. Constantly being on call or uncertain about shifts can disrupt work-life balance, strain personal relationships, and contribute to stress and anxiety.

Inequality and Inequity: Zero-hour contracts are more likely to affect vulnerable individuals, such as those in lower-income brackets, young people, and individuals from marginalised communities. The lack of stable employment opportunities can perpetuate existing social and economic disparities, exacerbating inequality.

It's important to note that there are differing views on zero-hour contracts, with some arguing they offer flexibility and opportunities for certain individuals. However, concerns regarding the negative impact on workers' well-being and employment rights have led to calls for greater regulation and reduction in the prevalence of these contracts.

There are several reasons why a better standard of shift patterns is needed in the security industry in the UK. Here are a few key considerations:

Fatigue and Performance: Security personnel often work long hours and irregular shifts, which can lead to fatigue. Fatigue impairs cognitive functioning, decision-making abilities, and reaction times, which can compromise security operations. By implementing better shift patterns, with adequate rest breaks and reasonable working hours, the industry can enhance the alertness and performance of security personnel.

Safety and Security: Fatigue-related errors can have serious consequences in the security industry. Security personnel play a critical role in protecting people, property, and assets. Fatigue can diminish their ability to detect and respond to security threats effectively, jeopardising the safety and security of individuals and organisations. Implementing better shift patterns can help mitigate these risks.

Work-Life Balance: Irregular shift patterns often make it challenging for security personnel to maintain a healthy work-life balance. Long working hours, including night shifts and weekend rotations, can disrupt family and social life, leading to increased stress and reduced job satisfaction. By introducing more balanced and predictable shift patterns, the industry can support the well-being and retention of security professionals.

Recruitment and Retention: The security industry faces ongoing challenges in recruiting and retaining skilled personnel. Unattractive shift patterns and demanding working conditions can deter individuals from pursuing security careers or lead to high turnover rates. By offering better shift patterns that prioritise reasonable working hours and rest periods, the industry can improve its appeal and enhance employee retention.

Legal and Compliance Requirements: The UK has specific laws and regulations governing working hours, rest breaks, and employee welfare. Ensuring compliance with these regulations is crucial to avoid legal issues and penalties. Implementing better shift patterns can help organisations meet these legal requirements and demonstrate their commitment to the well-being of their workforce.

Overall, improving shift patterns in the security industry can address issues of fatigue, enhance performance, promote work-life balance, support recruitment and retention efforts, and ensure compliance with legal and regulatory frameworks. By prioritising the well-being and effectiveness of security personnel, the industry can ultimately enhance its overall security capabilities.

Standards of Security Officers

It's important to note that security officer standards can vary across different countries and organisations within those countries. While it may be a perception that the standards of security officers are low in the UK, it would be inaccurate to make a blanket statement about the entire industry.

That being said, there can be several factors that might contribute to a perception of low standards in any given context:

Licensing and Regulations: The requirements and regulations for security officers can vary. If the licensing or certification process is not stringent or if the industry lacks comprehensive regulations, it can lead to variations in the quality of security officers.

Training and Education: The quality and extent of training programs available to security officers can have an impact on their competence and professionalism. Inadequate training programs or lack of emphasis on continuous professional development may contribute to lower standards.

Wages and Working Conditions: The compensation and working conditions for security officers can influence the level of motivation, commitment, and professionalism in the job. If wages are low or working conditions are unfavourable, it might attract individuals with lower qualifications or discourage those with higher skills and aspirations.

Recruitment and Selection Processes: The effectiveness of recruitment and selection processes can significantly impact the quality of security officers. If there are deficiencies in the recruitment process, such as inadequate background checks or limited screening, it could lead to the hiring of individuals who may not be suitable for the role.

Perception and Public Image: Public perception plays a role in shaping the standards and expectations of any profession. If security officers are not valued or their importance is not widely recognised, it can contribute to a lack of investment in training and development.

It's worth noting that these factors are not unique to the UK and can apply to security officer standards in various countries. Efforts to address these issues typically involve strengthening regulations, improving training programs, enhancing recruitment processes, and promoting the professionalisation of the security industry as a whole.

It's essential to recognise that the situation may have evolved since my last update, and specific incidents or reforms may have influenced the standards of security officers in the UK. For the most accurate and up-to-date information, I recommend referring to authoritative sources or conducting further research on recent developments in the security industry in the UK.

Improving the standards of security officers in the UK involves several key aspects, including training, professionalism, oversight, and ongoing development. Here are some steps that can be taken to enhance the standards of UK security officers:

Strengthen Training Programs: Enhance the training programs for security officers to ensure they have the necessary skills and knowledge to handle various situations effectively. This should include training on conflict resolution, emergency response, first aid, customer service, and relevant laws and regulations.

Implement Licensing and Certification: Introduce a licensing and certification system for security officers, which requires them to meet specific standards and undergo regular assessments. This can help ensure that individuals working as security officers are properly trained and qualified.

Promote Professionalism: Encourage security officers to uphold high professional standards by providing clear guidelines on appearance, conduct, and ethics. Emphasise the importance of customer service, communication skills, and respectful interactions with the public.

Increase Oversight and Accountability: Strengthen regulatory oversight and monitoring of security companies and officers. Regular audits, inspections, and performance evaluations can help identify areas for improvement and maintain accountability within the industry.

Foster Collaboration and Information Sharing: Establish platforms for security companies, industry associations, and law enforcement agencies to share best practices, exchange information, and collaborate on addressing emerging security challenges. This can enhance the overall effectiveness of security operations.

Support Continuing Professional Development: Encourage security officers to engage in continuous professional development to stay updated on the latest industry trends, technologies, and techniques. Provide opportunities for training workshops, seminars, and certifications to help them improve their skills and knowledge.

Enhance Communication and Reporting: Develop standardised reporting mechanisms to ensure effective communication between security officers, their supervisors, and relevant authorities. Encourage security officers to report incidents, concerns, and suspicious activities promptly, enabling timely response and appropriate action.

Embrace Technological Advancements: Invest in advanced security technologies, such as surveillance systems, access control systems, and alarm systems, to augment the capabilities of security officers. Provide training on how to use these technologies effectively.

Establish Mentoring Programs: Implement mentoring programs where experienced security officers can guide and support new recruits. This can help transfer knowledge, promote best practices, and foster a culture of continuous improvement within the security industry.

Engage in Stakeholder Collaboration: Engage with stakeholders, such as government agencies, private sector organisations, and the public, to gather feedback, address concerns, and develop strategies for enhancing security officer standards. Consider establishing advisory committees or forums to facilitate this collaboration.

By implementing these measures, the UK can enhance the professionalism, effectiveness, and overall standards of security officers, ultimately improving public safety and security.

Reports

When considering whether security reports should be done online-only in the UK, there are several factors to consider. Here is a pro for conducting security reports online:

Accessibility and Convenience: Online reporting provides a convenient and accessible method for individuals to submit security reports. It eliminates the need for physical visits or phone calls, allowing people to report incidents from anywhere with an internet connection. This convenience can encourage more individuals to report security concerns promptly, leading to a potentially quicker response from authorities.

However, it's important to note that there are also potential drawbacks and considerations when relying solely on online reporting. These include issues related to digital literacy, privacy and security concerns, and the need for alternative reporting channels for those who may not have internet access or prefer traditional methods. Ultimately, a balanced approach that considers different reporting options may be more suitable to cater to a diverse range of users.

Whether security reports should be done online-only or in-person in the UK depends on a variety of factors, such as the nature of the security concern, the urgency of the report, and the policies and procedures of the organisation or agency responsible for receiving the report.

In general, reporting security concerns online can be a convenient and efficient way to communicate important information quickly. Online reporting systems can allow individuals to submit reports 24/7, from anywhere with an internet connection, and provide a record of the report that can be easily tracked and monitored.

However, there may be situations where an in-person report is more appropriate. For example, if the security concern involves physical safety or an immediate threat, it may be necessary to report the concern in person to law enforcement or emergency services.

Ultimately, the decision of whether to report a security concern online-only or in-person should be based on the specific circumstances of the situation. If you are unsure how to report a security concern, you may want to consult with the organisation or agency responsible for receiving the report to determine the best course of action.

Why Security Needs Non-Disclosure Agreements and Confidentiality Acts

When implementing non-disclosure agreements (NDAs) and confidentiality acts for new officers, here are some steps to consider:

Clearly Define the Scope: Determine the specific information that needs to be protected and the extent to which it should remain confidential. This can include trade secrets, proprietary information, customer data, intellectual property, and any sensitive company information.

Draft Comprehensive Agreements: Develop well-drafted NDAs and confidentiality agreements that outline the obligations and responsibilities of the officers regarding the protection of confidential information. It should cover the duration of the agreement, the consequences of breaching it, and any specific requirements or restrictions.

Tailor Agreements to Roles: Customise the agreements to fit the specific roles and responsibilities of the officers. Different positions may require different levels of access to sensitive information, so ensure that the agreements are appropriate for each individual.

Provide Clear Explanations: During the onboarding process, thoroughly explain the importance of confidentiality and the consequences of breaching the agreement. Educate the officers about the potential risks to the company and its stakeholders if confidential information is disclosed.

Obtain Signed Agreements: Require officers to sign the NDAs and confidentiality agreements before they gain access to any sensitive information. Retain a copy of the signed agreement for future reference.

Access Controls and Monitoring: Implement robust access controls to ensure that officers only have access to the information necessary for their roles. Regularly review and update access permissions based on changing responsibilities. Implement monitoring mechanisms to detect any unauthorised access or suspicious activities.

Training and Awareness: Conduct regular training sessions and awareness programs to reinforce the importance of confidentiality. Keep officers informed about evolving threats, best practices, and legal obligations concerning the protection of confidential information.

Termination Protocols: Establish protocols for handling the termination or departure of officers. Clearly define the steps to be taken to ensure the return or destruction of any confidential information in their possession.

Ongoing Compliance: Continuously monitor and enforce compliance with the agreements. Regularly review and update the agreements to align with changing business needs and legal requirements.

Seek Legal Advice: It is advisable to consult with legal professionals to ensure that the NDAs and confidentiality agreements are legally sound and enforceable in your jurisdiction.

Remember, these steps provide general guidance, and it is important to consult with legal professionals and tailor the agreements to your organisation's specific requirements and local laws.

Improvements to the Vetting Process

Improving the vetting process for security officers in the UK is crucial to ensuring the safety and reliability of these individuals. Here are some suggestions to enhance the vetting process:

Standardise Vetting Procedures: Establish clear and standardised vetting procedures across all security organisations. This ensures consistency and eliminates discrepancies in the vetting process.

Comprehensive Background Checks: Conduct thorough background checks on prospective security officers. This includes verifying their identity, checking criminal records, employment history, and contacting references. Consider collaborating with law enforcement agencies and the Disclosure and Barring Service (DBS) for comprehensive criminal record checks.

Enhanced Interview Process: Conduct detailed interviews to assess the candidate's suitability for the role. Ask specific questions about their experience, motivations, and ability to handle challenging situations. It is essential to evaluate their communication skills, problem-solving abilities, and judgment.

Psychometric Assessments: Utilise psychometric assessments to evaluate the candidate's psychological suitability for the security officer role. These assessments can measure personality traits, cognitive abilities, and behavioural tendencies relevant to the job.

Financial Checks: Consider conducting financial checks to ensure that prospective security officers are not under undue financial stress or susceptible to bribery or corruption. This can involve checking credit history and examining any previous financial irregularities.

Reference Verification: Thoroughly verify the references provided by the candidate. Contact previous employers, supervisors, or colleagues to gather insights into the candidate's performance, reliability, and character.

Ongoing Training and Development: Implement a framework for continuous training and professional development for security officers. This ensures they stay up to date with evolving security practices, technology, and regulations. Regular training can also enhance their ethical conduct and decision-making skills.

Collaboration with Intelligence Agencies: Foster collaboration between security organisations and intelligence agencies to exchange relevant information and identify potential risks. This can help identify any red flags or connections to individuals or groups of concern.

Regular Reviews and Audits: Conduct periodic reviews and audits of the vetting process to identify areas for improvement. Consider involving independent auditors or third-party organisations to ensure impartiality and adherence to best practices.

Continuous Evaluation: Establish mechanisms for continuous evaluation of security officers' performance, conduct, and adherence to ethical standards. This can include regular performance reviews, customer feedback, and incident reporting.

By implementing these measures, the vetting process for security officers in the UK can be strengthened, ensuring that only qualified and trustworthy individuals are employed in these critical roles.

Using a credit check as part of vetting a new security officer in the UK can be considered problematic due to several reasons:

Relevance to the Job Role: Credit checks are typically used to assess an individual's financial history and creditworthiness. However, for a security officer position, financial status may not be directly relevant to their ability to perform the job. It is important to focus on qualifications, experience, and skills that directly relate to security duties, such as physical fitness, knowledge of security protocols, and decision-making abilities.

Discrimination Concerns: Credit checks have the potential to discriminate against individuals from disadvantaged backgrounds or those who have experienced financial difficulties. People may face financial challenges due to various factors such as medical expenses, unemployment, or family issues. Assessing candidates based on their credit history can disproportionately affect certain demographic groups and perpetuate socioeconomic inequalities.

Privacy and Data Protection: Conducting credit checks involves accessing an individual's sensitive financial information. This raises concerns about privacy and data protection, as it involves the handling of personal data that is not directly relevant to the job. Under the General Data Protection Regulation

(GDPR) in the UK, employers must have a valid legal basis for processing personal data and must ensure that the data collected is necessary and proportionate to the purpose.

Potential for Fraud: Requesting credit information from candidates for security positions may create opportunities for fraudulent activities. Sharing personal financial information with unauthorised individuals or organisations can put applicants at risk of identity theft or other forms of fraud. This can harm the applicants and damage the reputation of the organisation conducting the checks.

Instead of relying on credit checks, it is generally more appropriate to focus on other relevant aspects of vetting security officers, such as their criminal records, employment history, references, and qualifications. These factors provide a more accurate assessment of an individual's suitability for the role while minimising potential discrimination and privacy concerns.

Basic Training Changes

When it comes to training security officers for their new job in the UK, there are several basic changes that can be implemented to enhance their effectiveness and preparedness. Here are some suggestions:

Legal and Regulatory Knowledge: Provide comprehensive training on the relevant UK laws, regulations, and standards pertaining to security operations. This includes understanding the Private Security Industry Act 2001, Data Protection Act 2018, and General Data Protection Regulation (GDPR). Ensuring officers are aware of their legal obligations helps them operate within the boundaries of the law.

Threat Awareness and Risk Assessment: Train officers to identify potential threats and conduct risk assessments effectively. Teach them to recognise suspicious behaviour, identify potential security vulnerabilities, and report incidents promptly. This includes training on techniques for observing, monitoring, and assessing risks in various settings.

Conflict Resolution and De-escalation Techniques: Emphasise the importance of effective communication and conflict resolution skills. Provide training on de-escalation techniques to handle challenging situations without resorting to force. This helps officers maintain a calm and professional demeanour while ensuring public safety.

First Aid and Emergency Response: Equip officers with basic first aid skills and knowledge of emergency response protocols. This includes training in cardiopulmonary resuscitation (CPR), administering first aid in common emergencies, and understanding evacuation procedures. First aid and emergency response training can save lives and mitigate risks.

Technology and Digital Security: As technology continues to advance, it's crucial to train security officers in the effective use of relevant security tools and digital systems. Provide training on CCTV monitoring, access control systems, alarm systems, and other security-related technologies. Additionally, educate officers about cybersecurity best practices to protect sensitive information and digital assets.

Customer Service and Professionalism: Highlight the importance of delivering excellent customer service while maintaining a professional demeanour. Security officers often interact with the public, and their behaviour reflects on the organisations they represent. Training in effective communication, conflict resolution, and positive engagement helps officers build trust and create a safe environment.

Cultural Sensitivity and Diversity Training: Foster an inclusive environment by providing cultural sensitivity and diversity training. Teach officers to respect and accommodate individuals from different backgrounds, ethnicities, and cultures. This training helps officers better understand and serve diverse communities while preventing discrimination or bias incidents.

Practical Training Exercises: Implement realistic scenarios and practical training exercises to simulate real-world situations. This could include role-playing exercises, simulated emergency response drills, and scenarios involving conflict resolution. Hands-on training enhances officers' ability to apply their knowledge effectively.

Continual Professional Development: Encourage officers to engage in ongoing professional development and provide resources for further learning. This can include seminars, workshops, online courses, and industry conferences. Promoting continuous learning helps officers stay updated with new security techniques, technologies, and best practices.

Mental Health and Well-Being: Recognise the importance of mental health and well-being for security officers. Offer training on stress management, emotional resilience, and self-care. Support systems, such as access to counselling services or peer support networks, can also be established to ensure officers' well-being.

By incorporating these changes into the basic training of security officers in the UK, their overall preparedness, professionalism, and effectiveness can be significantly enhanced.

Security devices should be a part of a security officer's basic training in the UK for several reasons:

Enhanced Security Measures: Security devices play a crucial role in enhancing overall security measures. By including training on security devices, officers gain a deeper understanding of how these devices function, their limitations, and how to leverage them effectively to maintain a secure environment. This knowledge empowers officers to identify potential vulnerabilities and implement appropriate measures to mitigate risks.

Effective Monitoring and Surveillance: Security devices such as CCTV cameras, access control systems, and alarm systems are commonly used in various settings. By including training on these devices, security officers can learn how to operate and monitor them effectively. This enables them to detect suspicious activities, respond to emergencies, and prevent security breaches.

Incident Response and Management: Security devices often play a crucial role in incident response and management. By training security officers on the operation and usage of these devices, they can effectively coordinate with other security personnel and law enforcement agencies during emergencies. This includes providing real-time information from security devices, using two-way communication systems, and taking appropriate actions based on the situation.

Crime Prevention and Deterrence: The presence of security devices acts as a deterrent to potential criminals. When security officers are trained in the proper utilisation of these devices, they can proactively monitor and respond to suspicious behaviour. This proactive approach, combined with the effective use of security devices, helps to prevent crimes from occurring and maintain a safe environment.

Legal Compliance: Security officers must adhere to legal and regulatory requirements related to privacy, data protection, and surveillance. By including training on security devices, officers can develop an understanding of these regulations and ensure that their use of devices complies with the law. This knowledge helps to protect individuals' privacy rights while maintaining an appropriate level of security.

In summary, incorporating security device training into the basic training of security officers in the UK is essential to equip them with the necessary skills to effectively operate, monitor, and respond to security incidents. This training enhances overall security measures, improves incident response capabilities, and ensures compliance with relevant regulations.

There are several reasons why a security company in the UK might choose to conduct their own basic training for new security officers:

Standardisation: By developing their own training program, a security company can ensure that all their officers receive consistent and standardised training. This helps maintain a high level of competence and professionalism among their staff.

Tailored to Company Needs: Each security company may have its own unique requirements and expectations for its security officers. By conducting their own training, companies can customise the curriculum to align with their specific needs and operational procedures.

Company-Specific Policies and Protocols: Security companies often have their own set of policies, protocols, and standard operating procedures (SOPs) that govern their operations. Training new officers in-house allows the company to familiarise them with these internal guidelines from the outset.

Control Over Quality: By taking charge of the training process, a security company can directly oversee the quality and effectiveness of the training provided to its officers. This allows them to ensure that the training meets industry standards and adequately prepares officers for their roles.

Industry-Specific Knowledge: Security companies possess specialised knowledge and expertise relevant to their specific sectors, such as retail, event security, or corporate security. Conducting their own training enables them to incorporate this industry-specific knowledge into the curriculum, providing officers with the skills and knowledge necessary for their particular roles.

Cost Considerations: Outsourcing training to external providers can be expensive, especially if a company has a large number of officers to train. Developing an in-house training program can be a cost-effective solution in the long run, as it eliminates the need for external training fees.

Faster Onboarding: In-house training allows security companies to streamline the onboarding process for new officers. They can design training programs that focus specifically on the skills and knowledge required for their operations, enabling officers to quickly adapt to their roles and start working efficiently.

Company Culture and Values: In-house training provides an opportunity for security companies to instil their desired company culture and values in their officers right from the beginning. It allows them to emphasise important aspects such as professionalism, integrity, and customer service, which are integral to the company's brand identity.

It's worth noting that while many security companies conduct their own basic training, they still need to ensure that the training meets the legal requirements and standards set by regulatory bodies such as the Security Industry Authority (SIA) in the UK. Compliance with industry regulations is crucial to ensure that the training provided is valid and recognised within the security industry.

Why Security Companies Should Check on Their Officer Skills

Security companies should regularly check on their officers' skills for several important reasons:

Ensuring Competence: Regular skill assessments help security companies ensure that their officers possess the necessary knowledge, abilities, and training to perform their duties effectively. By verifying their skills, companies can ensure that their officers are competent and capable of handling various security challenges.

Risk Mitigation: Security officers are responsible for protecting people, property, and assets. If an officer lacks essential skills or knowledge, it can jeopardise the safety and security of the clients they serve. Regular skill checks enable companies to identify any skill gaps and take appropriate measures to address them, minimising the risk of security breaches or incidents.

Compliance with Regulations: In many jurisdictions, security companies are required to adhere to specific regulations and standards. These may include licensing requirements, training criteria, or industry certifications. By assessing officers' skills, companies can ensure compliance with such regulations and avoid legal or operational consequences.

Professional Development: Skill assessments provide security officers with opportunities for professional development. By identifying areas for improvement, officers can receive targeted training and education to enhance their skills. This not only benefits the individual officers but also contributes to the overall competence and quality of the security company.

Client Satisfaction: Clients hire security companies to receive reliable and efficient security services. Regularly assessing officers' skills helps maintain high service standards, ensuring client satisfaction. Companies that consistently demonstrate their commitment to maintaining skilled and capable officers are more likely to attract and retain clients.

Adaptation to Evolving Threats: The security landscape is constantly evolving, with new threats and challenges emerging regularly. Regular skill checks allow security companies to assess their officers' readiness to handle evolving threats and equip them with updated knowledge and techniques. This adaptability is crucial for providing effective security solutions in an ever-changing environment.

Employee Motivation and Engagement: Skill assessments can serve as a positive motivation tool for security officers. When companies invest in their officers' skill development and regularly evaluate their capabilities, it demonstrates a commitment to their professional growth. This can boost officer morale, job satisfaction, and overall engagement, leading to a more motivated and dedicated workforce.

By regularly checking on their officers' skills, security companies can enhance their overall effectiveness, maintain compliance with regulations, and provide high-quality security services to their clients, while also fostering a culture of continuous improvement within their organisation.

Basic Security Officer Training

Providing basic training to security officers is essential for several reasons, including:

Enhanced Security: Providing basic training to security officers helps them understand their roles and responsibilities better, which, in turn, leads to better security. With proper training, security officers are better equipped to identify potential security risks, take appropriate measures to mitigate them, and respond effectively to security incidents.

Improved Customer Service: Security officers are often the first point of contact for customers and visitors to a company. By providing basic training, companies can ensure that their security officers are polite, helpful, and approachable, creating a positive impression of the company and improving customer satisfaction.

Compliance with Regulations: Many industries have regulations that require security officers to have certain levels of training. For example, security officers in the healthcare industry must have training on patient privacy regulations. By providing basic training, companies can ensure that their security officers meet regulatory requirements.

Reduced Liability: In the event of a security incident, companies may be held liable for any damages or injuries that occur. By providing basic training, companies can reduce their liability by demonstrating that they took reasonable steps to prevent the incident from occurring.

Overall, providing basic training to security officers is a sound investment for companies as it can lead to enhanced security, improved customer service, regulatory compliance, and reduced liability.

There are several reasons why companies in the UK should not solely rely on the basic SIA (Security Industry Authority) training for security officers:

Limited Scope: The basic SIA training covers only the minimum requirements for security officers to obtain an SIA licence. This training provides a basic understanding of the role of a security officer, including basic security procedures and legislation. However, it does not cover specialised skills and knowledge that may be required for specific industries or environments.

Lack of Practical Experience: While the basic SIA training includes a practical component, it may not provide enough real-world experience for security officers to handle complex security situations. This could result in security officers being ill-equipped to handle incidents such as theft, vandalism, or even violent attacks.

Evolving Security Threats: The security industry is constantly evolving, and security officers must stay up to date with the latest security threats and countermeasures. Basic SIA training may not cover emerging security risks such as cyberattacks, terrorism, or sophisticated criminal activities.

Customer Expectations: Customers hiring security officers often have high expectations for professionalism, customer service, and specialised knowledge related to their industry or environment. Basic SIA training may not provide security officers with the necessary skills and knowledge to meet these expectations.

Legal Liabilities: Companies that rely solely on basic SIA training for their security officers may be exposing themselves to legal liabilities if security incidents occur due to inadequate training or preparation.

Therefore, it is essential for companies in the UK to ensure that their security officers receive additional specialised training and ongoing professional development to provide effective security services and meet the evolving needs of their customers.

Training new security officers after they get their SIA (Security Industry Authority) licence is crucial for companies in the UK for several reasons:

Enhancing Skills: The SIA licence is the basic requirement for working in the security industry in the UK. However, it only covers the essential skills and knowledge needed to perform basic security duties. Further training can enhance the officers' skills, knowledge, and confidence, enabling them to perform their duties more efficiently and effectively.

Keeping Up with the Latest Regulations: The security industry is constantly evolving, and new regulations are regularly introduced to address emerging threats. Companies that provide additional training to their security officers can ensure that they are up to date with the latest regulations and can adapt to changes in the industry.

Improved Performance: Additional training can help security officers to perform their duties better. They can learn new techniques and strategies for managing challenging situations, handling conflicts, and ensuring the safety and security of the premises and people they are responsible for.

Building Trust with Clients: Clients are more likely to trust a company that invests in its security officers' training and development. It demonstrates that the company takes security seriously and is committed to providing the best possible service to its clients.

Retention and Morale: Providing additional training opportunities can improve employee morale and job satisfaction, which can lead to better retention rates. Security officers who feel valued and supported by their employer are more likely to remain loyal to the company and deliver better performance.

In summary, training new security officers after they obtain their SIA licence is essential for companies in the UK to ensure their security officers are equipped with the necessary skills and knowledge to perform their duties efficiently and effectively. It can also help build trust with clients, improve employee morale and retention, and keep up with the latest regulations.

While online training can be a valuable tool for companies, it shouldn't be the sole source of employee training and development. Here are some reasons why:

Limited Interaction: Online training lacks the face-to-face interaction and collaboration that traditional training methods provide. This can make it more difficult for employees to ask questions, clarify concepts, and get feedback, leading to a less effective learning experience.

Lack of Personalisation: Online training courses are typically designed for a broad audience, which may not meet the specific needs of individual employees. Personalised training plans can help employees focus on the areas where they need the most improvement and lead to better outcomes.

Reduced Engagement: Employees may be less engaged during online training sessions because they can easily get distracted by other tasks or lose interest in the material. In-person training sessions are typically more engaging and can help keep employees focused on the learning objectives.

Limited Hands-On Experience: Some types of training, such as safety training or technical skills training, require hands-on experience. This can be difficult to replicate in an online environment, making it less effective than in-person training.

Limited Networking Opportunities: Traditional training methods, such as conferences and workshops, provide valuable networking opportunities that online training cannot replicate. These opportunities allow employees to learn from others in their field, build relationships, and gain insights that they may not have otherwise.

Overall, while online training can be a useful tool for companies, it should be part of a larger training and development program that includes other types of training, such as in-person sessions and on-the-job training.

Having a dedicated person responsible for site training and updating officer training can be highly beneficial for companies in a number of ways:

Ensuring Consistency: A dedicated training officer can help ensure that new officers receive consistent training across different sites, departments, and teams. This can help reduce confusion and errors, and ensure that all officers are following the same procedures and best practices.

Keeping Up with Changes: A training officer can stay up to date with changes in policies, procedures, and technology, and ensure that officers are trained on the latest techniques and tools. This can help improve efficiency, effectiveness, and safety, and reduce the risk of accidents or mistakes.

Retention: Training officers can help improve officer retention by providing ongoing support and training opportunities, and helping officers develop their skills and careers. This can help boost morale and job satisfaction, and reduce turnover and recruitment costs.

Compliance: A training officer can ensure that officers are trained on all relevant laws, regulations, and industry standards, and help the company stay in compliance with these requirements. This can help reduce the risk of legal or financial penalties, and protect the company's reputation.

Overall, having a dedicated person responsible for site training and updating officer training can help companies improve their operations, reduce risk, and achieve their business goals more effectively.

Here are some of the airers that I think companies need to make sure the new and old officers know, and companies keep their officers up to date with the training.

What Skills a Security Officer Needs

In the UK, a security officer typically requires a range of skills to perform their duties effectively. Here are some essential skills for a security officer in the UK:

Security Knowledge: A security officer should have a solid understanding of security principles, procedures, and protocols. They should be familiar with security systems, access control, surveillance techniques, and emergency response procedures.

Communication Skills: Effective communication is crucial for a security officer. They need to be able to communicate clearly and confidently with colleagues, clients, and members of the public. Good verbal and written communication skills are essential for documenting incidents, writing reports, and providing clear instructions.

Observational Skills: Security officers must possess keen observational skills to identify potential security threats, suspicious activities, or unauthorised access. They should be attentive to detail, able to spot unusual behaviour or signs of criminal activity, and capable of assessing risks.

Conflict Resolution: De-escalating conflicts and resolving disputes is an important aspect of a security officer's role. They should be trained in conflict resolution techniques, such as effective communication, negotiation, and problem-solving, to handle tense situations professionally and prevent violence.

Physical Fitness and Stamina: Security officers may be required to patrol large areas, stand for long periods, or respond to physical altercations. Being physically fit and having good stamina is important to carry out their duties effectively.

Integrity and Trustworthiness: Security officers are entrusted with maintaining the safety and security of people and property. They should demonstrate high levels of integrity, ethics, and reliability. Trustworthiness is vital as security officers often handle confidential or sensitive information.

First Aid and Emergency Response: Having knowledge of first aid and emergency response procedures is essential. Security officers may need to provide initial medical assistance in case of injuries or medical emergencies and should be trained in basic life-saving techniques.

Technology Literacy: Security officers often work with security systems, surveillance cameras, access control systems, and other technology tools. Familiarity with these systems and the ability to use them effectively is important for efficient operation and monitoring.

Teamwork: Security officers often work as part of a team, collaborating with colleagues, supervisors, law enforcement, or emergency services. Being able to work effectively in a team environment and follow instructions is crucial for coordinated security efforts.

Legal and Regulatory Knowledge: Security officers should have a good understanding of relevant laws, regulations, and guidelines related to their duties. This includes knowledge of the Security Industry Authority (SIA) licensing requirements and codes of practice.

It's worth noting that specific skills and requirements can vary depending on the type of security officer role, such as retail security, event security, corporate security, or residential security. Additional specialised training may be necessary for certain sectors or positions.

Why It Important to Keep a Security Daily Occurrence Book

Keeping a security daily occurrence book is important for several reasons:

Record-Keeping: A security daily occurrence book serves as a record of all security-related incidents that occur within a particular period. This information can be used for future reference, such as when conducting investigations, reviewing security procedures, or identifying patterns of security breaches.

Compliance: Some organisations are required by law or regulation to keep a security daily occurrence book. This is especially true for entities that handle sensitive information or assets, such as financial institutions, hospitals, and government agencies.

Liability: A security daily occurrence book can help protect an organisation from liability in the event of a security breach or incident. By documenting all incidents, an organisation can demonstrate that it took appropriate steps to address security concerns and minimise potential harm.

Training and Education: A security daily occurrence book can serve as a training and educational tool for security personnel. By reviewing past incidents and identifying areas for improvement, security personnel can develop strategies to prevent future incidents and respond more effectively to security threats.

Overall, keeping a security daily occurrence book is an important part of any organisation's security program and can help promote a culture of security awareness and preparedness.

What Information Is Needed for a Report Form

When filling out an incident report form, it's important to provide accurate and detailed information to ensure that the incident is properly documented. Here are some steps to follow:

Provide Your Personal Information: Start by filling out your name, job title, and contact information.

Describe the Incident: Describe the incident in detail, including the date, time, and location. Be as specific as possible about what happened, who was involved, and any witnesses.

Provide a Narrative: Write a narrative describing the sequence of events leading up to the incident, what occurred during the incident, and any actions taken after the incident. Use clear and concise language and avoid opinions or speculation.

Identify Any Injuries or Damages: If anyone was injured or property was damaged, document this information in the report. Include the extent of the injuries or damage and any medical treatment or repairs that were required.

Include Any Supporting Documentation: If you have any photographs, diagrams, or other documents related to the incident, attach them to the report.

Sign and Date the Report: Once you have completed the report, sign and date it to verify that the information is accurate and complete.

Remember that incident reports are used to document incidents for future reference and to identify any areas where improvements can be made. Therefore, it's important to provide as much detail as possible to ensure that the incident is properly documented.

Why Should Security Know the Fire and Alarm Procedures

Security personnel should know the fire and alarm procedures for several important reasons:

Emergency Response: In the event of a fire or other emergency, security personnel may be the first ones on the scene. Knowing the fire and alarm procedures will enable them to respond quickly and effectively, minimising the risk of harm to people and property.

Evacuation Procedures: Security personnel play a key role in ensuring that building occupants are safely evacuated in the event of a fire or other emergency. Knowing the fire and alarm procedures will enable them to guide people to the nearest exit, muster point or assembly area, and ensure that everyone is accounted for.

Preventing False Alarms: Security personnel can help prevent false alarms by ensuring that people do not misuse or tamper with fire detection and alarm systems. Knowing the fire and alarm procedures will enable them to educate people about proper use of the systems and to take appropriate action when false alarms occur.

Compliance with Regulations: Building codes and fire safety regulations require that security personnel receive training on fire and alarm procedures. Knowing the procedures will help ensure that the building is in compliance with these regulations, reducing the risk of fines and legal liability.

Overall, knowing the fire and alarm procedures is essential for security personnel to effectively protect people and property in the event of a fire or other emergency.

This will change depending on the site you are on.

Why Security Officers Need to Do Check Calls

A check call is a routine communication process used by security personnel to confirm their location and status to the control room. This is an important security measure that helps to ensure the safety of the personnel and the premises they are protecting. There are several reasons why security personnel need to do a check call to the security control room, including:

Ensuring Personnel Safety: By checking in with the control room at regular intervals, security personnel can confirm that they are safe and sound. This is particularly important in high-risk situations or when working alone.

Maintaining Situational Awareness: Check calls help the control room maintain situational awareness of what is happening on the ground. If a security guard fails to check in, the control room can take appropriate action to ensure their safety.

Responding to Emergencies: If a security guard encounters an emergency situation, such as a fire, medical emergency, or criminal activity, they can quickly call for assistance from the control room.

Confirming Security Protocols: Check calls also help to ensure that security protocols are being followed. For example, if a guard is supposed to be patrolling a certain area, the check call confirms that they are indeed in that area and carrying out their duties.

Overall, check calls are an important part of a comprehensive security plan, helping to ensure the safety of personnel and the premises they are protecting.

This will depend on the site you are on.

How to Do a Security Handover

A security officer should follow the following steps to do a site handover at the end of their shift:

Conduct a Final Patrol of the Site: Before starting the handover process, the security officer should do a final patrol of the site to ensure that everything is secure and there are no ongoing issues that need to be addressed.

Meet with the Incoming Security Officer: The outgoing security officer should meet with the incoming security officer to provide a comprehensive briefing on the site's current security status, any incidents or issues that occurred during the shift, and any relevant information that the incoming officer should be aware of.

Review the Site Logbook: The outgoing security officer should review the site logbook and ensure that it is up to date and accurate. Any incidents or issues that occurred during the shift should be documented in the logbook.

Hand Over Any Equipment: The outgoing security officer should hand over any equipment, such as keys, radios, and other devices, to the incoming officer and ensure that they are in good working order.

Confirm the Handover: Before leaving the site, the outgoing security officer should confirm with the incoming officer that they have all the information they need and that they understand their responsibilities for the shift.

Sign Off: The outgoing security officer should sign off on the handover, indicating that they have completed all necessary tasks and provided all relevant information to the incoming officer.

By following these steps, the security officer can ensure a smooth and effective site handover at the end of their shift.

Why a Security Officer Should Read the Site Assignment Instruction Book

The reasons why a security officer in the UK may be advised to read the site assignment instruction book. While specific practices and requirements may vary, here are some general benefits:

Familiarity with Site-Specific Procedures: The site assignment instruction book contains essential information about the specific location where the security officer is assigned to work. It outlines the site's security protocols, emergency procedures, access control measures, and other critical instructions unique to that site. Reading the book helps the officer understand and adhere to the specific protocols required for that location.

Compliance with Regulations: Security officers are responsible for maintaining a safe and secure environment in accordance with local laws and regulations. The site assignment instruction book often contains legal requirements, industry standards, and guidelines that security officers must follow. By reading the book, officers can ensure they are compliant with these regulations and perform their duties effectively.

Threat Assessment and Risk Management: Understanding the potential risks and threats specific to a site is crucial for effective security management. The site assignment instruction book may outline potential threats, vulnerabilities, and risk mitigation strategies relevant to that location. By reading the book, security officers can better assess the risks associated with their assigned site and take appropriate preventive or responsive actions.

Emergency Response Preparedness: In the event of an emergency, security officers play a vital role in maintaining order, protecting lives, and minimising damage. The site assignment instruction book typically includes detailed emergency response procedures, such as evacuation plans, communication protocols, and contact information for relevant authorities. By familiarising themselves with these procedures, officers can respond effectively and efficiently during emergencies.

Client Expectations and Service Delivery: Security officers often work on behalf of a client or organisation that has specific expectations and requirements for their site's security. The site assignment instruction book may contain information about the client's preferences, unique requests, or specific protocols they want security officers to follow. Reading the book helps officers understand and meet these expectations, ensuring high-quality service delivery.

It's important to note that practices and guidelines may vary depending on the organisation, site, or security provider. Thus, it is essential for security officers to consult their supervisors or management for specific instructions regarding reading and adhering to the site assignment instruction book.

Why Is It Important to Keep a Training Record for Security Officers

Keeping a training record for security officers in the UK is important for several reasons:

Compliance: Security officers are required to undergo specific training to meet regulatory requirements and industry standards. Maintaining training records ensures that security officers are appropriately trained and compliant with legal obligations, such as those set out in the Private Security Industry Act 2001 and the Security Industry Authority (SIA) licensing requirements.

Accountability: Training records serve as evidence of the training received by security officers. In case of any incidents or allegations, the records can demonstrate that the officer has undergone the necessary training to perform their duties effectively and responsibly. It helps establish a system of accountability and assists in addressing any concerns related to the officer's competence or actions.

Performance Evaluation: Training records provide a means to assess the performance and competence of security officers. By tracking their training progress and certifications, employers can evaluate the skills, knowledge, and capabilities of each officer. This evaluation can aid in identifying areas for improvement, providing targeted training, and ensuring the ongoing professional development of security personnel.

Quality Assurance: Maintaining training records supports quality assurance efforts within the security industry. It enables organisations to ensure consistent training standards across their workforce, verifying that all officers receive the required training and possess the necessary skills to perform their duties effectively. By establishing and maintaining high training standards, the overall quality of security services can be enhanced.

Continuity and Succession Planning: Training records facilitate continuity and succession planning within security organisations. They provide a clear overview of the training history and qualifications of individual officers. This information is valuable for identifying potential candidates for promotion or specialised roles within the security team, ensuring a smooth transition and maintaining the required skill sets within the organisation.

Overall, maintaining training records for security officers in the UK is crucial for compliance, accountability, performance evaluation, quality assurance, and effective management of security personnel. It supports the delivery of high-quality security services and helps build trust and confidence in the industry.

Why Should Security Officers Be Trained on UK COSSH

Security officers should be trained in UK Control of Substances Hazardous to Health (COSHH) regulations for several reasons:

Knowledge of Hazards: Security officers may come into contact with various hazardous substances while performing their duties. These substances could include cleaning chemicals, solvents, fuels, or other dangerous materials. Training in COSHH helps security officers understand the risks associated with these substances, their potential health effects, and the appropriate measures to mitigate those risks.

Risk Assessment: COSHH training equips security officers with the skills to conduct proper risk assessments. They learn how to identify hazardous substances, assess their potential impact on individuals and the environment, and implement control measures to minimise exposure. This knowledge allows security officers to proactively address risks and take appropriate action to prevent accidents, spills, or incidents.

Emergency Response: In the event of a hazardous substance spill or incident, security officers trained in COSHH are better prepared to respond effectively. They understand the appropriate actions to take to ensure their own safety, as well as the safety of others in the vicinity. This could include evacuating the area, alerting emergency services, containing the spill, or providing immediate assistance to affected individuals.

Compliance with Regulations: COSHH is a legal requirement in the UK under the Control of Substances Hazardous to Health Regulations 2002. By ensuring security officers are trained in COSHH, organisations demonstrate their commitment to complying with these regulations. It helps create a safer working environment and reduces the risk of regulatory penalties or legal liabilities resulting from non-compliance.

Communication and Cooperation: COSHH training fosters better communication and cooperation between security officers and other staff members who may handle hazardous substances. Security officers can effectively liaise with relevant personnel, such as cleaning staff or facilities management, to ensure proper handling, storage, and disposal of hazardous materials. This collaboration promotes a culture of safety throughout the organisation.

Overall, training security officers in UK COSHH regulations enhances their ability to recognise, assess, and manage risks associated with hazardous substances. It promotes a safer working environment, ensures compliance with legal obligations, and improves emergency response capabilities.

Why a Security Officer Should Have a Basic Understanding of the UK GDPR

A security officer should have a basic understanding of the UK General Data Protection Regulation (GDPR) because it plays a crucial role in safeguarding personal data and ensuring compliance with data protection laws. Here are several reasons why a security officer should possess this knowledge:

Data Protection Responsibilities: Security officers are often involved in handling and protecting personal data within an organisation. Understanding the UK GDPR enables them to grasp their responsibilities regarding data protection, including the security measures required to safeguard personal data from unauthorised access, loss, or misuse.

Legal Compliance: The UK GDPR sets out the legal framework for data protection in the United Kingdom. Security officers need to be aware of the regulation's key provisions, rights of individuals, and organisational obligations. By having a basic understanding of the UK GDPR, security officers can ensure that their organisation adheres to the law, mitigating the risk of legal consequences such as fines and penalties for non-compliance.

Data Breach Management: In the event of a data breach or security incident, security officers play a vital role in incident response and mitigation. The UK GDPR mandates that organisations promptly report certain types of breaches to the relevant authorities and affected individuals. Understanding the requirements for breach notification is crucial for security officers to take appropriate actions in such situations.

Privacy by Design and Default: The UK GDPR emphasises the principle of "privacy by design and default", which requires organisations to integrate data protection measures into their systems and processes from the outset. Security officers should understand the concept and ensure that security controls and measures are implemented throughout the organisation's infrastructure, applications, and services.

Data Subject Rights: The UK GDPR grants individuals various rights concerning their personal data, such as the right to access, rectification, erasure, and restriction of processing. Security officers should understand these rights to assist individuals who may exercise them and ensure that the organisation has processes in place to handle such requests appropriately.

Data Transfer and International Considerations: The UK GDPR covers the transfer of personal data outside the United Kingdom and the European Economic Area (EEA). Security officers should be familiar with the provisions and requirements related to international data transfers, such as adequacy decisions, standard contractual clauses, and binding corporate rules.

Overall, a security officer with a basic understanding of the UK GDPR can effectively contribute to an organisation's data protection efforts, implement appropriate security measures, and ensure compliance with data protection regulations.

UK Law for Security Officers on Searching Motor Vehicles

As an AI language model, I can provide you with general information on the topic, but it's important to note that laws can change over time, so it's always a good idea to consult the most up-to-date legal sources or seek professional advice for specific legal matters.

In the UK, the powers of security officers to search motor vehicles are limited compared to those of the police. Security officers employed by private organisations typically do not have the same authority as police officers when it comes to searching vehicles.

Private security officers may have the power to conduct searches on private property, such as shopping centre car parks, but their authority is derived from the property owner or occupier rather than from specific legal powers. The extent of their search powers would typically be outlined in their employment contract or guidelines provided by their employer.

If a security officer wishes to search a motor vehicle, they generally need the consent of the vehicle owner or driver. Refusing to consent to a search by a security officer does not constitute a criminal offence in itself, although the security officer may deny entry to the premises or take other appropriate actions within the scope of their employment.

It's important to distinguish the powers of private security officers from those of the police. Police officers in the UK have broader search powers under various legislation, such as the Police and Criminal Evidence Act 1984 (PACE) and the Terrorism Act 2000, which grant them specific authority to stop and search vehicles in certain circumstances.

If you require precise information about the legal powers of security officers in a specific context or jurisdiction within the UK, it is advisable to consult relevant statutes, legal professionals, or the specific guidelines of the organisation employing the security officers.

UK Law on Searching Someone

In the UK, security officers have the power to search individuals under certain circumstances. The power to search is usually granted by the property owner or the organisation that employs the security officer.

If the security officer has been granted the power to search individuals, they must follow specific guidelines when conducting the search. These guidelines are outlined in the Private Security Industry Act 2001 and the Code of Practice on Searching Persons.

Here are some key points to keep in mind regarding searches conducted by security officers in the UK:

The security officer must have reasonable grounds to suspect that the person being searched is carrying prohibited items, such as weapons or drugs.

The security officer must provide their name, the name of the company they work for, and the reason for the search.

The search must be conducted in a private area and with a person of the same gender as the individual being searched.

The security officer must use the least intrusive method possible when conducting the search.

The individual being searched has the right to refuse the search, but this may result in the person being denied entry to the premises.

The security officer must provide a written record of the search, including the reason for the search, the date and time of the search, and any items found.

It's important to note that the power to search individuals is only granted to security officers who have been trained and licensed to perform this task. If you feel that your rights have been violated during a search conducted by a security officer, you should contact the police or seek legal advice.

How Security Officers Should Search Motor Vehicles in the UK

In the UK, security officers may need to search motor vehicles in certain circumstances, such as at airports, border crossings, or high-security facilities. While I can provide some general guidelines, it's important to note that specific procedures and legal requirements may vary depending on the context and the organisation for which the security officers work. It's always best to consult the guidelines and policies set forth by the relevant authorities or institution. That being said, here are some general considerations for searching motor vehicles in the UK.

Legal Authority: Security officers should have the legal authority to conduct vehicle searches. This authority may stem from legislation, specific regulations, or their employment contract. Ensure that the search is conducted within the boundaries of the law and the scope of the authority provided.

Justification and Consent: There should be a valid reason for conducting the search, such as suspicion of illegal activity or a security threat. In some cases, obtaining the driver's or owner's consent may be necessary, while in other situations, specific legislation might grant the authority to search without consent, such as at border checkpoints.

Safety Precautions: Prioritise personal safety during the search. Maintain situational awareness, be alert for potential risks or threats, and call for backup or assistance if needed. If a vehicle search poses a significant risk, it may be appropriate to delay or conduct the search in a controlled environment.

Methodology: When searching a motor vehicle, security officers should employ a systematic and thorough approach. Some key areas to focus on include the trunk, passenger compartments, glove compartment, and any storage compartments. Pay attention to concealed spaces or compartments that may be used to hide illicit items.

Respect and Professionalism: Interact with the driver and passengers respectfully and professionally throughout the search process. Explain the purpose of the search, answer their questions to the extent allowed, and handle their belongings with care.

Documentation: Maintain detailed records of the search, including the date, time, location, the name(s) of the officer(s) involved, reason for the search, and any findings or outcomes. This documentation may be required for legal purposes or to maintain an audit trail.

Disposal of Personal Information: If personal information unrelated to the search is inadvertently discovered (e.g., documents, identification cards), treat it with confidentiality and respect. Avoid unauthorised disclosure or misuse of such information.

Consistency and Fairness: Apply search procedures consistently and fairly to all individuals to avoid any perception of bias or discrimination. Treat individuals with dignity and respect, regardless of their background or appearance.

Remember, these guidelines are meant to provide general information and may not cover all specific circumstances. It is important to consult the relevant legislation, organisational policies, and training materials to ensure compliance with legal requirements and best practices.

Searching of a Woman

It is important for me to emphasise that body-searching a person, especially a woman, is a sensitive and potentially invasive process that must be conducted with great care and respect for the individual's privacy and dignity. It is critical to ensure that security personnel who are responsible for conducting body searches are appropriately trained and follow established protocols and guidelines to minimise the risk of any harm or discomfort to the person being searched.

Here are some general guidelines that can be helpful in training security officers in conducting body searches:

Establish Clear and Concise Guidelines: Before any training begins, it is important to establish clear and concise guidelines for conducting body searches. These guidelines should be based on relevant laws and regulations, as well as industry best practices and protocols.

Explain the Importance of Privacy and Dignity: It is essential to emphasise the importance of respecting the individual's privacy and dignity during the search process. Security personnel must be trained to use professional language and behaviour, maintain a respectful demeanour, and communicate effectively with the individual being searched.

Demonstrate Proper Search Techniques: A trainer can demonstrate proper search techniques and provide opportunities for trainees to practice these techniques in a controlled environment. This should include a thorough explanation of the areas of the body that can be searched and the appropriate level of force that may be used.

Address Sensitivity and Cultural Differences: It is important to recognise that different people may have varying levels of sensitivity or cultural differences that must be considered during the search process. Trainers should emphasise the need for sensitivity and awareness in such situations and provide appropriate guidance to security personnel.

Provide Ongoing Training and Evaluation: Ongoing training and evaluation are critical to ensuring that security personnel continue to perform body searches in a professional and respectful manner. Regular feedback and assessments can help identify areas for improvement and ensure that personnel are following established guidelines.

In summary, training security officers in body-searching a woman should emphasise the importance of respecting privacy and dignity, demonstrate proper search techniques, address sensitivity and cultural differences, and provide ongoing training and evaluation. It is essential to approach this process with care and sensitivity to ensure that the person being searched is treated with the utmost respect and professionalism.

Searching of a Man

Body-searching a man is a sensitive and important task that requires proper training to ensure that it is done safely, effectively, and in a manner that respects the individual's dignity and privacy. Here are some steps to train someone in body-searching a man:

Explain the Legal and Ethical Considerations: Start by explaining the laws and regulations governing body searches. It is essential to ensure that the searcher understands the legal and ethical implications of the search and the importance of respecting the person's rights and privacy.

Demonstrate the Technique: Once the searcher understands the legal and ethical considerations, demonstrate the proper technique for conducting a body search on a male subject. Show them how to use their hands and fingers to feel for objects and how to ensure that they do not miss any potential concealed items.

Provide Practice Scenarios: Once the searcher has seen the technique in action, provide them with practice scenarios to help them build confidence and familiarity with the technique. Start with simple scenarios and gradually increase the complexity as the searcher becomes more comfortable with the process.

Provide Feedback: During the practice scenarios, provide the searcher with feedback on their technique. Correct any mistakes or oversights and ensure that they are following proper protocol.

Ensure Safety: It is important to prioritise safety during the body search. Ensure that the searcher is using appropriate safety equipment and techniques to minimise the risk of injury to themselves or the subject.

Reinforce the Importance of Professionalism: Finally, emphasise the importance of maintaining professionalism and respect during the search. The searcher should avoid any behaviour that could be perceived as inappropriate or disrespectful.

Overall, training someone in body-searching a man requires patience, attention to detail, and a focus on safety and professionalism. By following these steps, you can help ensure that the searcher is well-equipped to handle this important task.

How a Security Officer Should Do
a Bag Search

In the UK, security officers may conduct bag searches for various reasons, primarily to ensure the safety and security of individuals and the premises they are entering. Here are some reasons why bag searches may be conducted by security officers:

Prevention of Unauthorised Items: Bag searches help prevent prohibited or unauthorised items from being brought into certain premises, such as airports, stadiums, concert venues, or government buildings. These items can include weapons, explosives, drugs, or other items that may pose a threat to public safety.

Deterrence and Detection of Theft: Bag searches can help deter and detect theft or smuggling of valuable items, both from within the premises and from other individuals' belongings. This is especially relevant in places like retail stores, where bag checks are done to prevent shoplifting.

Compliance with Security Protocols: Some organisations or institutions have specific security protocols in place that require bag searches as part of their standard operating procedures. This is often the case in high-security environments, such as military installations or sensitive government facilities.

Mitigation of Potential Risks: Bag searches are conducted as a precautionary measure to mitigate potential risks and maintain a safe environment. By checking the contents of bags, security officers can identify any suspicious or potentially dangerous items that may compromise the security or safety of the premises or the people inside.

It's important to note that bag searches should be conducted in accordance with the law and respect individual rights and privacy. In the UK, security officers must adhere to legal guidelines and policies, ensuring that searches are conducted fairly, impartially, and without discrimination.

Training in Bomb Threat Call in the UK Workplace

The general guidelines for handling bomb threats in the workplace:

Remain Calm: Stay composed and try to keep others around you calm as well.

Follow Protocols: If your workplace has specific procedures in place for handling bomb threats, follow them carefully. This may include notifying security personnel or management immediately.

Evacuation: If there is an immediate and credible threat, evacuate the building following established evacuation procedures. Do not use elevators and avoid crowded areas.

Contact Authorities: Dial the emergency services number (in the UK, it's 999) to inform the police about the situation. Provide them with all the necessary details and follow their instructions.

Document Information: If you receive a bomb threat call, try to gather as much information as possible. Take note of the exact words spoken, the caller's voice characteristics, and any background noises you can hear.

Do Not Confront the Caller: Avoid engaging with the caller or making any promises. Stay focused on gathering information and following necessary procedures.

Inform Management: Notify your immediate supervisor or a designated authority figure in your workplace about the bomb threat call. They will be responsible for coordinating with the relevant authorities and making decisions regarding the safety of employees.

Remember, every workplace may have specific guidelines and protocols in place for handling such situations, so it's important to be familiar with them in advance. Stay safe, and always prioritise personal safety and the safety of others.

Confiscating Items

In the UK, security officers are authorised to confiscate items under certain circumstances to maintain safety and security in public spaces and premises. The power to confiscate items is usually granted under specific laws or regulations, such as the Terrorism Act 2000, the Misuse of Drugs Act 1971, or the Prevention of Crime Act 1953.

Security officers may confiscate items that are considered to pose a threat to public safety, such as weapons, explosives, or dangerous chemicals. They may also confiscate items that are prohibited in certain areas, such as alcohol or drugs in a music festival or event. Additionally, security officers may confiscate items that are being used in a manner that could cause harm or damage, such as fireworks or laser pointers.

It's important to note that security officers must follow strict guidelines when confiscating items, and they must provide a clear reason for doing so. They should also provide a receipt for any items that are confiscated, and the owner of the item should be given clear instructions on how to retrieve it if it is not permanently seized.

If someone believes their property has been confiscated unlawfully, they should report it to the relevant authority or contact a solicitor for legal advice.

Security Officers Should Be Trained in First Aid at Work

In the UK, it is highly beneficial for security officers to be trained in first aid at work for several reasons:

Prompt Response to Emergencies: Security officers are often the first individuals to arrive at the scene of an incident or emergency, including accidents, injuries, or medical emergencies. Having first aid training equips them with the necessary skills to provide immediate assistance and stabilise the situation before professional medical help arrives. This can significantly improve the chances of positive outcomes and potentially save lives.

Duty of Care: Security officers have a duty of care towards the people they are responsible for protecting, such as employees, visitors, or customers in a facility. By having first aid skills, they can fulfil this duty more effectively. They can administer immediate first aid and minimise the severity of injuries or medical conditions until medical professionals take over.

Workplace Safety Compliance: The Health and Safety (First Aid) Regulations 1981 in the UK require employers to provide adequate first aid provisions in the workplace. This includes ensuring that there are trained individuals available to administer first aid in case of an emergency. By training security officers in first aid, employers can meet these legal requirements and create a safer working environment.

Rapid Intervention: Security officers are often positioned strategically throughout a facility, enabling them to respond quickly to incidents. Their presence allows them to quickly identify and react to potential accidents or injuries. By having first aid skills, they can provide immediate assistance, initiate CPR (cardiopulmonary resuscitation), control bleeding, or stabilise fractures, thus minimising the impact of injuries and potentially saving lives.

Enhanced Professionalism: First aid training enhances the professionalism of security officers. It demonstrates their commitment to providing a safe environment for employees, visitors, and customers. It also boosts confidence among the security team, enabling them to handle emergencies more effectively and efficiently.

Personal Safety: First aid training not only focuses on providing assistance to others but also teaches individuals how to assess risks and take appropriate safety precautions. Security officers trained in first aid are more likely to recognise potential hazards and take preventive measures, reducing the chances of accidents or injuries in the first place.

Overall, by training security officers in first aid at work, employers can enhance workplace safety, comply with legal requirements, and improve the overall well-being of individuals within their premises. It enables security officers to respond effectively to emergencies, minimise the severity of injuries, and create a safer environment for everyone.

Internal and External Site Patrols

Training someone to do a security patrol of a site inside and outside requires a combination of classroom instruction and hands-on training. Here are some steps you can follow:

Start with the Basics: Begin by explaining the importance of security patrols and the role they play in protecting the site. Discuss the potential risks and threats that the patrol officer may encounter during their patrol.

Review Site Layout and Hazards: Provide a comprehensive overview of the site layout, including all access points and potential entry points. Identify hazards that the patrol officer may encounter, such as uneven terrain, slippery surfaces, or obstacles that could obstruct their view.

Explain the Patrol Procedure: Walk the patrol officer through the patrol procedure, including the areas that need to be checked, the frequency of the checks, and any specific protocols that need to be followed. Be sure to explain the importance of maintaining a consistent pattern and checking all areas thoroughly.

Demonstrate Proper Use of Equipment: If the patrol officer will be using equipment such as flashlights, radios, or surveillance cameras, demonstrate proper use and handling of the equipment.

Practice Scenarios: Provide the patrol officer with hands-on training by practicing different scenarios that they may encounter during their patrol. For example, simulate a fire alarm going off, an intruder attempting to break in, or a medical emergency.

Emphasise the Importance of Documentation: Explain the importance of documenting all findings during the patrol, including any irregularities or incidents. Provide examples of the types of documentation that should be recorded, such as time stamps, location, and descriptions of any suspicious activities.

Provide Ongoing Training: Ongoing training is critical to ensure that the patrol officer remains up to date on the latest security protocols and procedures. Schedule regular training sessions to reinforce best practices and identify areas for improvement.

By following these steps, you can train someone to do a thorough and effective security patrol of a site inside and outside.

Handheld Metal Detector

Using a handheld metal detector in security requires proper training and adherence to established protocols to ensure effective and accurate screening.

Here are the steps to follow when using a handheld metal detector in security:

Familiarise Yourself with the Metal Detector: Before using a metal detector, make sure to read and understand the manufacturer's instructions and any specific protocols established by your organisation.

Prepare the Individual Being Screened: Inform the individual being screened that they will be scanned with a metal detector and ask them to remove any metal objects they may be carrying, such as belts, jewellery, or keys. If the individual cannot remove metal objects due to medical reasons, such as a pacemaker, inform the appropriate personnel to perform a secondary screening.

Conduct the Scan: Start by waving the metal detector over the individual's clothing, starting from the top of their body and moving downwards. Ensure you cover all areas of the body, including pockets, waistbands, and ankles. If the detector beeps, conduct a secondary search of the area where the alarm sounded.

Follow Up with Secondary Screening: If the metal detector detects any metal objects during the screening, inform the individual and request that they remove the object for secondary screening. If the individual refuses or cannot remove the object, inform the appropriate personnel to conduct a secondary screening.

Document the Screening: Record the results of the metal detector screening, including any objects detected and actions taken. This documentation can be helpful for tracking potential security incidents and for compliance with any relevant regulations.

Remember to remain calm and professional throughout the screening process, and communicate clearly with the individuals being screened. Following these steps can help ensure a safe and effective security screening process using handheld metal detectors.

Metal Detector Arch

Training someone to use a metal detector arch in security involves several steps that need to be followed carefully. Here are some general guidelines to help you get started:

Explain the Purpose of Metal Detector Arch: Start by explaining why metal detector arches are used in security and how they help in detecting metallic objects that may pose a threat to security.

Demonstrate How to Use the Metal Detector Arch: Show the trainee how to use the metal detector arch by walking through it yourself, and explaining the correct procedure step by step.

Provide Hands-On Practice: Give the trainee ample opportunity to practice using the metal detector arch under your supervision. Encourage them to ask questions and provide feedback to ensure they fully understand the process.

Explain the Indicators: Explain the different types of indicators that the metal detector arch provides when detecting metal objects, such as visual, audio, or vibrating alarms.

Provide Instruction on Searching Techniques: Provide instructions on how to search a person effectively by asking them to remove any metal objects from their pockets, belts, shoes, and any other items that may trigger the alarm.

Explain the Protocol for Handling Suspicious Objects: Train the user on the protocol for handling suspicious objects that may be detected during the search process.

Provide Ongoing Support: Provide ongoing support and regular training sessions to ensure that the trainee maintains their proficiency in using the metal detector arch.

Remember to emphasise the importance of being respectful and professional when using the metal detector arch, as this will help to maintain a positive and safe environment for everyone involved.

X-Ray Machine

Training someone to use an X-ray machine involves several steps to ensure that the operator can operate the machine safely and effectively. Here are the steps you can follow to train someone to use an X-ray machine:

Provide Basic Knowledge of X-Ray Technology: It's important to provide the trainee with a basic understanding of X-ray technology, including the physics behind it, how it works, the types of X-ray machines available, and their different uses. This knowledge will help the trainee to understand the importance of safety precautions.

Safety Training: Safety should be the number one priority when it comes to operating an X-ray machine. You should teach the trainee how to handle and store the equipment safely, and explain the safety protocols that need to be followed during the operation. This includes wearing proper protective gear, setting up the X-ray machine properly, and handling the radiation source with care.

Hands-On Training: Provide the trainee with hands-on training on how to operate the X-ray machine. This should include practicing positioning the patient and the equipment, selecting the appropriate settings, and operating the X-ray machine itself. The trainee should also be taught how to troubleshoot common problems that may arise during the operation of the machine.

Image Interpretation: The trainee should be trained on how to interpret X-ray images. They should learn how to identify normal and abnormal anatomy and how to recognise common pathological conditions.

Ongoing Training: The trainee should receive ongoing training to keep their knowledge and skills up to date. This should include continuing education courses, regular refresher training, and staying up to date with new advances in X-ray technology.

Overall, training someone to use an X-ray machine requires a combination of theoretical knowledge, hands-on training, and ongoing education to ensure they can safely and effectively operate the equipment.

Radio Training

Training someone in radio communications involves teaching them the basics of radio technology, the principles of radio communications, and the proper protocols for using radio equipment. Here are some steps you can follow to train someone in radio communications:

Introduce the Basics of Radio Technology: Start by explaining the basic principles of radio technology, including frequency, wavelength, modulation, and propagation. You can use diagrams and visual aids to help illustrate these concepts.

Explain Radio Communications Protocols: Teach the trainee the proper procedures for using radio equipment, including how to transmit and receive messages, how to use proper radio etiquette, and how to handle emergency situations.

Familiarise the Trainee with Radio Equipment: Show the trainee how to operate different types of radio equipment, including handheld radios, base stations, and repeaters. Explain how to tune the equipment and how to use different modes of operation.

Conduct Practical Exercises: Have the trainee practice sending and receiving messages using the radio equipment. Use scenarios that simulate real-life situations, such as responding to emergency calls or coordinating with other radio users.

Provide Feedback and Correction: Give the trainee feedback on their performance and provide corrective guidance as needed. Emphasise the importance of clear communication and proper etiquette when using radio equipment.

Test the Trainee's Knowledge: Test the trainee's understanding of radio communications by asking them to explain key concepts and procedures, and by having them perform practical exercises on their own.

By following these steps, you can effectively train someone in radio communications and ensure they are proficient in using radio equipment for various applications.

Security Officer Needs to Know How to Check UK Banknotes

Security officers need to know how to check UK banknotes for several reasons:

Prevention of Counterfeiting: The primary reason for checking banknotes is to detect counterfeit currency. Counterfeit notes can circulate in the economy, leading to financial losses for individuals and businesses. Security officers play a crucial role in identifying counterfeit banknotes and preventing their circulation.

Protection of Businesses: Security officers are often responsible for maintaining the security of businesses, including banks, retail stores, and other establishments that handle cash transactions. By being able to check the authenticity of UK banknotes, they can safeguard their organisations against financial losses resulting from counterfeit currency.

Maintaining Public Trust: Security officers are representatives of the institutions they work for, and their ability to identify genuine banknotes helps maintain public trust. When customers see that security officers are diligent in checking banknotes, it enhances their confidence in the business or institution.

Compliance with Legal Requirements: Financial institutions, such as banks, have legal obligations to prevent the circulation of counterfeit currency. Security officers help fulfil these obligations by verifying the authenticity of banknotes during cash handling processes.

Identifying Suspicious Activities: Security officers are trained to be vigilant and observant. They can identify patterns or individuals involved in suspicious activities related to counterfeit money. By recognising counterfeit banknotes, they can assist law enforcement agencies in investigating and apprehending individuals involved in counterfeiting operations.

To effectively check UK banknotes, security officers are trained in various security features incorporated into genuine currency, such as watermark, security thread, holograms, raised print, and UV ink. They learn about the specific characteristics of UK banknotes and use tools like UV lights, magnifying glasses, and counterfeit detection pens to aid in their inspection.

Security Officer Needs to Know How to Check UK Passport

As a security officer, there are several things you can do to check a passport to ensure its authenticity and the identity of the passport holder. Here are some steps you can follow:

Check the Cover: The cover of a genuine passport should be made of a durable, waterproof material and should have the country's name and emblem on it.

Look for Security Features: Modern passports have many security features, such as holograms, watermarks, microprinting, and UV-visible inks. Check for these features by shining a UV light on the passport, holding it up to the light, and examining it closely.

Check the Biographic Information: Look at the passport holder's name, photo, date of birth, and other personal information. Verify that the photo matches the person in front of you.

Check the Expiration Date: Make sure that the passport is not expired.

Verify the Passport Number: Look up the passport number in a database or contact the relevant embassy or consulate to verify that the passport is valid and hasn't been reported lost or stolen.

Watch for Signs of Tampering: Check for signs of tampering, such as glued pages, ripped or torn pages, or missing pages.

Ask Questions: Ask the passport holder some questions to verify their identity, such as their name, date of birth, and where they're travelling from and to.

If you have any doubts about the authenticity of a passport, you should escalate the issue to your supervisor or the relevant authorities.

Security Officer Needs to Know How to Check UK Driving Licence

As a security officer, there are a few ways to check the authenticity of a UK driving licence:

Check the driver's licence for any obvious signs of forgery or tampering. Look for signs such as misspellings, blurry text or images, or alterations to the licence.

Verify the driver's identity by checking their photo on the licence. Ensure that the person presenting the licence matches the photo on the licence.

Check the expiration date of the licence to ensure that it is still valid. You can also check the driver's age to ensure that they are old enough to drive.

Verify the licence number by contacting the Driver and Vehicle Licensing Agency (DVLA) in the UK. You can do this online or by phone using the DVLA's free licence checking service.

Consider using a specialised licence scanner or reader to quickly verify the licence's authenticity and check for any potential issues.

It's important to note that as a security officer, you may not be able to verify the licence with 100% certainty, and it's always a good idea to err on the side of caution and involve law enforcement or other appropriate authorities if you suspect any issues with a licence presented to you.

Difference Between Civil and Criminal Crime in the UK

A security officer in the UK should know the difference between civil and criminal crimes for several reasons:

Legal Responsibilities: Security officers are responsible for maintaining law and order within their jurisdiction. Understanding the distinction between civil and criminal crimes helps them effectively respond to and report incidents based on the appropriate legal framework.

Response and Intervention: Knowing the difference between civil and criminal offences enables security officers to respond appropriately to various situations. Criminal offences, such as theft or assault, require immediate intervention to protect lives and property, and security officers may need to collaborate with law enforcement agencies. Civil matters, such as contract disputes or property damage, may require a different approach, such as facilitating communication or documenting incidents for potential legal proceedings.

Reporting and Documentation: Security officers are often required to prepare incident reports and provide accurate information about the nature of the offence. Understanding whether an incident falls under civil or criminal law helps officers provide the necessary details and ensures the appropriate legal processes are followed.

Liability and Legal Protection: Security officers need to protect themselves and their organisations from legal liabilities. By recognising the difference between civil and criminal crimes, they can avoid overstepping their authority in civil matters, preventing potential legal consequences.

Collaboration with Law Enforcement: Security officers often work alongside law enforcement agencies. Understanding the legal distinctions between civil and criminal offences helps foster effective collaboration by enabling clear communication and coordination with police officers, ensuring appropriate actions are taken.

Conflict Resolution: Security officers may find themselves in situations where they need to mediate disputes between individuals or parties. Knowing the difference between civil and criminal offences allows them to guide parties towards the appropriate resolution processes, such as suggesting legal advice or alternative dispute resolution methods.

In summary, a security officer's knowledge of the difference between civil and criminal crimes in the UK is crucial for fulfilling their legal responsibilities, responding effectively to incidents, reporting and documenting offences accurately, protecting themselves and their organisation from liabilities, collaborating with law enforcement, and facilitating conflict resolution.

Security Officer Should Know De-Escalation Techniques

Security officers are often trained in de-escalation techniques for several reasons:

Conflict Management: Security officers are frequently exposed to situations that have the potential to escalate into physical altercations or violence. By learning de-escalation techniques, officers can effectively manage conflicts and diffuse tense situations before they escalate, reducing the risk of harm to themselves, others involved, and property.

Public Safety: Security officers are responsible for maintaining public safety and order within their designated areas. De-escalation techniques enable them to communicate effectively, assess situations accurately, and resolve conflicts without resorting to force. This helps in creating a safer environment for everyone involved.

Customer Service: Many security officers work in environments where they interact with the public, such as shopping malls, event venues, or residential complexes. Learning de-escalation techniques allows them to handle difficult or irate individuals with empathy and professionalism, defusing potential conflicts and providing better customer service.

Legal Compliance: Security officers must operate within the boundaries of the law and respect individuals' rights. De-escalation techniques emphasise non-violent approaches and encourage officers to exhaust all peaceful means before considering the use of force. This training helps officers understand legal requirements and promotes adherence to appropriate protocols.

Personal Safety: De-escalation techniques not only benefit those around security officers but also help protect the officers themselves. By learning to manage confrontations, defuse aggression, and resolve conflicts peacefully, security personnel can minimise personal risk and maintain their own safety while performing their duties.

Overall, the inclusion of de-escalation techniques in security officer training promotes professionalism, reduces violence, and enhances the ability to handle challenging situations effectively, ensuring the safety and well-being of all parties involved.

Why a Security Officer Needs to Be Able to Describe Someone

A security officer needs to be able to describe someone for several important reasons:

Identifying Suspects: If a security officer witnesses or is informed about a suspicious or criminal activity, they need to provide accurate descriptions of individuals involved. This information is crucial for identifying potential suspects and assisting law enforcement in apprehending them.

Communication with Colleagues: Security officers often work in teams or communicate with other staff members. Describing someone allows them to effectively communicate important details about a person's appearance or behaviour, enabling their colleagues to quickly recognise and respond to the situation.

Incident Reporting: Accurate descriptions of individuals involved in security incidents are essential for creating comprehensive incident reports. These reports serve as official records and may be used for legal and investigative purposes. A thorough and detailed description enhances the reliability and usefulness of these reports.

Public Safety and Assistance: Describing someone accurately is important when dealing with public safety issues or providing assistance to individuals in need. For instance, a security officer may need to describe a lost child, a missing person, or someone requiring medical attention. This information aids in effective communication with emergency services, improving the chances of a successful outcome.

Preventing Unauthorised Access: Security officers are responsible for monitoring access to restricted areas and ensuring only authorised personnel are granted entry. Being able to describe someone who appears suspicious or lacks proper identification assists in maintaining a secure environment by identifying potential security threats or unauthorised individuals.

In summary, the ability to describe someone accurately is vital for a security officer to perform their duties effectively, including identifying suspects, communicating with colleagues, generating incident reports, ensuring public safety, and preventing unauthorised access.

Security Officer Should Have Knowledge of Physical Intervention

A security officer should have knowledge of physical intervention for several important reasons:

Personal Safety: Physical intervention techniques help security officers protect themselves in potentially dangerous situations. They learn how to manage and control aggressive or violent individuals without causing harm to themselves or others. Understanding physical intervention allows officers to maintain their own safety while attempting to defuse a threatening situation.

Public Safety: Security officers are responsible for maintaining public safety in various environments, such as airports, malls, concerts, or sporting events. They may encounter individuals who pose a risk to the safety of others. With knowledge of physical intervention techniques, officers can effectively control and restrain individuals who may be a threat, minimising harm to innocent bystanders.

Conflict Resolution: Physical intervention techniques are not solely about overpowering or restraining individuals. They also encompass skills related to conflict resolution and de-escalation. Security officers trained in physical intervention learn how to communicate effectively, defuse tense situations, and use appropriate force only as a last resort. These skills help prevent incidents from escalating and promote a peaceful resolution.

Legal Compliance: Security officers must adhere to legal and ethical guidelines when it comes to physical intervention. By being knowledgeable in this area, officers can ensure that their actions align with local laws and regulations. They understand the principles of proportionality and use-of-force continuum, which guide them in determining the appropriate level of force to employ based on the threat level presented.

Emergency Response: In emergency situations, security officers may need to intervene physically to protect lives and property. This can include situations like active shooter incidents, where immediate action is required to neutralise the threat. Knowledge of physical intervention equips officers with the skills to respond effectively, potentially saving lives and mitigating further harm.

It's important to note that while physical intervention skills are valuable, security officers should always prioritise prevention, de-escalation, and non-violent approaches whenever possible. The goal is to maintain a safe and secure environment while minimising harm to all parties involved.

Why a Security Officer Should Know Body Language Basics

A security officer should know basic body language for several reasons:

Threat Detection: Body language can provide valuable cues about a person's intentions and emotional state. By observing body language, a security officer can identify signs of aggression, nervousness, deception, or suspicious behaviour. These indicators can help the officer assess potential threats and take appropriate action to maintain security.

Conflict De-escalation: Understanding body language can assist a security officer in de-escalating tense situations. By recognising signs of escalating aggression or agitation, they can respond calmly and defuse the situation before it becomes violent. Body language awareness allows officers to adapt their own demeanour and communication style to promote a more peaceful resolution.

Non-verbal Communication: Effective communication is crucial in security-related scenarios. Sometimes verbal communication may be limited or not possible due to noise, language barriers, or other factors. In such cases, body language becomes a vital tool for conveying messages and understanding the intentions of others. By interpreting gestures, facial expressions, posture, and other non-verbal cues, a security officer can enhance their ability to communicate effectively.

Observing Suspicious Activity: Body language can reveal important information about an individual's intentions or involvement in illicit activities. Security officers who are trained to recognise abnormal or incongruous behaviour can identify potential threats or criminal behaviour more easily. By paying attention to body language cues, officers can spot signs of nervousness, furtiveness, or attempts to conceal something, enabling them to intervene and prevent potential security breaches.

Situational Awareness: Body language is a key component of situational awareness. By actively observing the body language of individuals within a given environment, security officers can gain insights into the overall atmosphere and detect anomalies or potential risks. This heightened awareness allows officers to proactively address security concerns and take preventive measures.

Overall, having knowledge of body language basics empowers security officers to be more perceptive, proactive, and effective in their roles, ultimately contributing to a safer and more secure environment.

Security Officer Should Have Knowledge of Terrorism Awareness

A security officer should have knowledge of terrorism awareness for several important reasons:

Threat Identification: Terrorism is a significant global threat, and security officers play a vital role in preventing and mitigating potential attacks. By having knowledge of terrorism awareness, security officers can identify suspicious activities, behaviours, or indicators that may suggest a terrorist threat. This includes recognising suspicious packages, monitoring unusual behaviour, and identifying potential weapons or explosive devices.

Prevention and Deterrence: Security officers are often the first line of defence in protecting people, property, and assets. Understanding terrorism awareness enables them to implement effective preventive measures and deter potential attackers. By recognising vulnerabilities and implementing appropriate security protocols, security officers can help create a safer environment and reduce the risk of terrorist incidents.

Emergency Response: In the unfortunate event of a terrorist attack, security officers are responsible for coordinating and implementing emergency response procedures. Knowledge of terrorism awareness equips them with the necessary understanding of different attack methods, response tactics, and evacuation procedures. This knowledge enables security officers to respond swiftly, effectively, and in collaboration with law enforcement agencies.

Public Safety and Communication: Security officers often interact with the public, and having knowledge of terrorism awareness allows them to communicate and educate individuals about potential threats. They can provide guidance on recognising and reporting suspicious activities, enhancing public safety awareness, and ensuring that appropriate authorities are informed in a timely manner.

Collaboration with Law Enforcement: Security officers frequently work in conjunction with law enforcement agencies. Their understanding of terrorism awareness facilitates effective communication and collaboration with law enforcement personnel during potential threats or incidents. By speaking a common language and sharing relevant information, security officers can support law enforcement efforts in preventing or responding to terrorism-related activities.

Preparedness and Training: Knowledge of terrorism awareness helps security officers to be better prepared for potential threats. Training programs that cover terrorism awareness provide them with essential skills, such as threat assessment, risk analysis, emergency response, and crisis management. By staying informed and updated on emerging trends, tactics, and threats, security officers can maintain a high level of preparedness and adapt their strategies as needed.

Overall, the knowledge of terrorism awareness is crucial for security officers to fulfil their role effectively, enhance public safety, prevent attacks, and respond appropriately during potential incidents. By being proactive, vigilant, and well-informed, security officers contribute significantly to the security and well-being of the communities they serve.

Why a Security Officer Should Always Ask for Some ID

A security officer should always ask for some form of identification as part of their responsibilities to maintain a secure and safe environment. Here are some reasons why it is important:

Verification of Identity: Asking for ID helps verify the identity of individuals entering a premise or seeking access to certain areas. By checking identification, security officers can ensure that individuals are who they claim to be. This helps prevent unauthorised access and potential security breaches.

Access Control: Many facilities have restricted areas where only authorised personnel are allowed. Requesting ID helps security officers determine whether individuals have the necessary authorisation to enter such areas. It enables them to enforce access control policies effectively and prevent unauthorised personnel from gaining entry.

Guest Management: In situations where visitors or guests are present, asking for ID allows security officers to track and monitor who is entering and exiting the premises. This helps create an accurate record of visitors and aids in managing any potential security incidents or investigations.

Deterrence and Prevention: The mere act of requesting ID can act as a deterrent to individuals with malicious intent. It sends a message that security measures are in place and that unauthorised access will not be tolerated. Potential wrongdoers may be less likely to attempt any unlawful activities if they know they will be required to provide identification.

Compliance with Policies and Regulations: In many industries and organisations, there are legal and regulatory requirements regarding identification checks for security purposes. Security officers must adhere to these policies to maintain compliance and ensure the safety of the premises and its occupants.

Emergency Situations: In the event of an emergency, having accurate identification information about individuals present on the premises can be crucial. It helps emergency responders and security personnel identify and locate individuals, especially if evacuation or accountability measures are necessary.

It is important to note that security officers should handle personal identification information responsibly and in accordance with applicable privacy laws and regulations.

Security Officer Should Have Their Observational Skills Checked

Security officers play a critical role in maintaining safety and security within various environments, such as airports, malls, banks, and other public or private spaces. Observational skills are essential for security officers because they allow them to effectively identify and respond to potential threats or suspicious activities. Here are several reasons why security officers should have their observational skills regularly checked:

Threat Detection: Observational skills enable security officers to spot unusual or suspicious behaviour, identify potential threats, and take appropriate action. By honing their observation skills, security officers can better detect signs of criminal activity, such as theft, vandalism, or individuals acting in a suspicious manner.

Prevention of Security Breaches: Strong observational skills empower security officers to proactively identify vulnerabilities in security protocols or physical infrastructure. By paying attention to details, they can detect weaknesses in access control systems, surveillance blind spots, or breaches in perimeter security, allowing for prompt remedial action.

Emergency Response: During emergencies, such as fires, medical incidents, or security breaches, security officers are often the first to respond. By having well-developed observational skills, they can quickly assess the situation, provide accurate information to emergency responders, and take appropriate measures to protect people and property.

Crowd Management: In crowded environments, security officers must monitor large groups of people effectively. By honing their observational skills, they can identify potential conflicts, signs of distress, or suspicious activities within a crowd. This allows them to intervene proactively and prevent situations from escalating.

Gathering Evidence: Observational skills are crucial when gathering evidence for investigations. Security officers who can observe and remember details accurately can provide valuable information to law enforcement or internal investigators. Their ability to recall specific events, descriptions of individuals, or actions can significantly contribute to solving crimes or resolving security incidents.

Proactive Risk Assessment: By continuously honing their observational skills, security officers can actively assess and mitigate potential risks. They can identify patterns of behaviour, recognise trends in criminal activity, and implement preventive measures accordingly. This proactive approach helps to minimise security threats and maintain a safe environment.

Regularly checking and training security officers' observational skills ensures that they remain sharp, vigilant, and capable of fulfilling their responsibilities effectively. It allows them to adapt to evolving security challenges, improves their situational awareness, and enhances their ability to protect people and property.

Conclusion: Why Is the SIA Good and Bad for the UK Security Industry

The Security Industry Authority (SIA) is a regulatory body in the United Kingdom that oversees and licences individuals working in the private security industry. The SIA plays a crucial role in enhancing the overall security landscape of the UK. Here are some reasons why the SIA is considered good for the UK security industry:

Professionalism and Standards: The SIA sets high standards for individuals working in the security industry, ensuring that they possess the necessary skills, qualifications, and integrity to perform their roles effectively. This promotes professionalism and enhances the overall quality of security services provided in the UK.

Public Safety: By regulating the private security industry, the SIA helps to safeguard public safety. Licensed security professionals undergo background checks, which reduces the risk of individuals with criminal backgrounds working in the sector. This enhances public trust and confidence in security personnel.

Improved Industry Reputation: The SIA's licensing scheme helps to weed out rogue operators and unqualified individuals from the security industry. This leads to an improved industry reputation, as customers can trust that licensed security providers meet the required standards and adhere to a code of conduct.

Crime Prevention: The SIA's role in vetting and licensing security personnel contributes to crime prevention. Trained and qualified security professionals are better equipped to identify potential threats, respond to incidents, and deter criminal activity. This aids in maintaining public safety and reducing crime rates.

Collaboration with Law Enforcement: The SIA works closely with law enforcement agencies to share information, intelligence, and best practices. This collaboration helps in tackling security challenges effectively and promotes a coordinated approach to maintaining security within the UK.

Economic Benefits: The private security industry is a significant contributor to the UK economy. By ensuring professionalism and high standards, the SIA supports the growth and development of the industry. Licensed security providers attract business investments, both domestically and internationally, which leads to job creation and economic prosperity.

Training and Development: The SIA encourages continuous professional development within the security industry. It promotes training programs, certification, and skills enhancement, which benefits security personnel by providing them with opportunities for career advancement and improving their competence in handling security-related tasks.

In conclusion, the SIA's role in regulating and licensing individuals working in the UK security industry brings numerous benefits. It promotes professionalism, public safety, crime prevention, collaboration with law enforcement, economic growth, and the overall development of security personnel. These factors make the SIA a valuable asset for the UK security industry.

Some points have been raised by critics regarding the Security Industry Authority (SIA) and its impact on the UK security industry.

Excessive Regulation: Critics argue that the SIA's regulatory framework imposes unnecessary burdens on businesses and individuals working in the security industry. The licensing requirements, fees, and bureaucratic processes can be seen as barriers to entry, making it difficult for smaller businesses and individuals to participate in the industry.

Limited Effectiveness: Some argue that the SIA's licensing scheme doesn't necessarily guarantee the quality of security services provided. Critics claim that the focus on obtaining a licence may overshadow the importance of other factors, such as experience, training, and practical skills. They believe that alternative approaches, such as industry-led self-regulation or more stringent training standards, could be more effective in ensuring quality.

Cost and Administrative Burden: The licensing fees and associated administrative costs required by the SIA are often cited as a burden for security companies. These additional expenses can place financial strain on businesses, particularly smaller firms. Critics argue that such costs are ultimately passed on to clients, potentially leading to higher service charges or limiting the availability of security services.

Lack of Flexibility: The SIA's regulatory framework may be seen as inflexible and slow to adapt to changes in the industry. Critics argue that emerging technologies and evolving security challenges require more agile responses. The rigid licensing system may not adequately address new areas of security, such as cyber security or technological advancements, where specialised skills are in demand.

Ineffective Enforcement: Some critics question the SIA's effectiveness in enforcing compliance with licensing regulations. They argue that resources could be better allocated to activities such as training and education, rather than focusing primarily on licensing and monitoring.

It's worth noting that while there are criticisms, the SIA was established to enhance professionalism and standards of the UK security industry, ensuring public safety and confidence. Proponents of the SIA argue that regulation is necessary to maintain quality and accountability within the industry. Ultimately, the assessment of the SIA's impact on the UK security industry depends on individual perspectives and experiences.

www.ingramcontent.com/pod-product-compliance
Lightning Source LLC
Chambersburg PA
CBHW072214170526
45158CB00002BA/601